# Soulful Connections

## Exploring the Intersection of Religion and Spirituality

**Meshari Alkulaib**

© **Copyright 2023 - All rights reserved.**

The content contained within this book may not be reproduced, duplicated or transmitted without direct written permission from the author or the publisher.

Under no circumstances will any blame or legal responsibility be held against the publisher, or author, for any damages, reparation, or monetary loss due to the information contained within this book, either directly or indirectly.

Legal Notice:

This book is copyright protected. It is only for personal use. You cannot amend, distribute, sell, use, quote or paraphrase any part, or the content within this book, without the consent of the author or publisher.

Disclaimer Notice:

Please note the information contained within this document is for educational and entertainment purposes only. All effort has been executed to present accurate, up to date, reliable, complete information. No warranties of any kind are declared or implied. Readers acknowledge that the author is not engaged in the rendering of legal, financial, medical or professional advice. The content within this book has been derived from various sources. Please consult a licensed professional before attempting any techniques outlined in this book.

By reading this document, the reader agrees that under no circumstances is the author responsible for any losses, direct or indirect, that are incurred as a result of the use of the information contained within this document, including, but not limited to, errors, omissions, or inaccuracies.

# Table of Contents

**INTRODUCTION** .................................................................................. 1

**CHAPTER 1: THE SACRED PATRIARCH ABRAHAM** ............................... 7
- ABRAHAM'S CALL AND COVENANT ............................................................. 8
- TEST OF SACRIFICE .................................................................................. 10
- FATHER OF NATIONS ............................................................................... 11
- ABRAHAM'S JOURNEY AND MIGRATIONS ................................................. 12
  - *Origin in Ur of the Chaldeans* .............................................................. 13
  - *Journey to Canaan* .............................................................................. 14
  - *Sojourn in Egypt* ................................................................................. 15
  - *Wells, Altars, and Nomadic Life* .......................................................... 16
- ABRAHAM'S RELATIONSHIP WITH GOD ..................................................... 17
- KEY TAKEAWAYS ...................................................................................... 18

**CHAPTER 2: ONE GOD, MANY PATHS** ............................................... 21
- MONOTHEISM AS THE CORE BELIEF .......................................................... 22
- CONCEPTIONS OF GOD ............................................................................. 24
- CREATION OF THE UNIVERSE AND HUMANITY ........................................... 26
- DIVINE REVELATION AND TRANSCENDENCE .............................................. 27
- MORALITY AND WORSHIP ........................................................................ 29
- KEY TAKEAWAYS ...................................................................................... 30

**CHAPTER 3: SACRED TEXTS—TORAH, BIBLE, AND QURAN** ................. 33
- THE TORAH .............................................................................................. 33
- THE BIBLE ................................................................................................ 34
- THE QURAN ............................................................................................. 37
  - *The Traditional Muslim Perspective* ..................................................... 37
  - *Supporting the Quran's Authenticity* .................................................... 38
- CORE TEACHINGS AND MORAL VALUES .................................................... 39
  - *Ethical Teachings of Judaism* ............................................................... 40
  - *Christian Values and Christian Life* ...................................................... 42
  - *Core Islamic Values* ............................................................................. 44

**CHAPTER 4: MESSENGERS OF DIVINE WISDOM** ................................ 47

- Role and Function of the Prophets .................................................. 47
- Key Prophets in Judaism ............................................................... 50
- Key Prophets in Christianity ........................................................... 52
- Key Prophets in Islam .................................................................... 54
- Signs and Miracles ........................................................................ 56

## CHAPTER 5: CONNECTING WITH THE DIVINE THROUGH PRAYER AND RITUAL ........................................................................................ 59

- Forms and Times of Prayer ........................................................... 59
  - Jewish Prayers ......................................................................... 60
  - Christian Prayers ..................................................................... 62
  - Muslim Prayers ....................................................................... 65
- Rituals of Purification .................................................................. 67
- Sacred Spaces and Places ............................................................ 69
  - Jewish Worship and Sacred Sites ............................................. 70
- Christian Worship and Sacred Sites .............................................. 71
  - Christian Holy Sites ................................................................. 71
- Islamic Worship and Sacred Sites ................................................. 72
  - Mosque Architecture .............................................................. 72
  - Significant Islamic Holy Sites ................................................... 73
- Role of Chanting and Recitation ................................................... 74
  - Benefits of Chanting ............................................................... 74
- Christian Chants: Tranquility and Divine Connection ..................... 75
- Chanting the Path to Unity: The Power of Jewish Chants ............... 75

## CHAPTER 6: SPIRITUAL JOURNEY SEEKING GOD'S PRESENCE ........ 77

- Inner Transformation .................................................................. 78
- Judaism: Spiritual Disciplines ....................................................... 80
- Islamic Disciplines ....................................................................... 82
- The Role of Faith ......................................................................... 84
- From Belief to Faith ..................................................................... 85
- Definition of Faith in Islam ........................................................... 86
- Practices of Self-Reflection .......................................................... 87
- Challenges and Tests ................................................................... 88

## CHAPTER 7: MORAL PRINCIPLES AND ETHICAL VALUES ................ 91

- Justice and Fairness .................................................................... 91
- Honesty and Integrity .................................................................. 94
- Respect for Life ........................................................................... 97
- Humility and Humbleness ............................................................ 98
- Forgiveness and Reconciliation .................................................... 99

GENEROSITY AND CHARITY .................................................................. 100
SINCERITY IN PRAYER AND WORSHIP ..................................................... 101

## CHAPTER 8: COMMUNITY AND COMMUNAL WORSHIP ................... 103

IMPORTANCE OF COMMUNITY ............................................................. 104
COMMUNAL WORSHIP PRACTICES ......................................................... 106
FESTIVALS AND CELEBRATIONS ............................................................. 108
SPIRITUAL GUIDANCE AND LEADERSHIP ................................................ 110
COMMUNAL ETHICS AND ACCOUNTABILITY ........................................... 112

## CHAPTER 9: SOCIAL JUSTICE AND MORAL RESPONSIBILITY .............. 115

ADVOCACY FOR THE MARGINALIZED ..................................................... 115
MUSLIMS MARGINALIZED IN THE UNITED STATES ................................... 117
PEACEMAKING AND CONFLICT RESOLUTION .......................................... 119
OPPOSITION TO INJUSTICE ................................................................... 120
POVERTY ALLEVIATION ........................................................................ 122
GLOBAL RESPONSIBILITY ...................................................................... 124

## CHAPTER 10: BRIDGING DIFFERENCES THROUGH INTERFAITH DIALOGUE .................................................................................... 127

IMPORTANCE OF INTERFAITH DIALOGUE ............................................... 128
SHARED BELIEFS AND VALUES .............................................................. 130
INTERPRETING SACRED TEXTS .............................................................. 132
EXPLORING THEOLOGICAL DIFFERENCES .............................................. 134
SEVEN THINGS CHRISTIANS, JEWS, AND MUSLIMS SHARE ...................... 135
OVERCOMING STEREOTYPES AND PREJUDICE ....................................... 137

## CHAPTER 11: LOVE AND COMPASSION—UNIVERSAL SPIRITUAL PRINCIPLES .................................................................................. 141

LOVE AS THE CORE PRINCIPLE ............................................................. 142
DIVINE PRINCIPLES TO STRENGTHEN YOUR RELATIONSHIPS ................... 144
THE CONCEPT OF LOVE FOR GOD ......................................................... 146
THE IMPORTANCE OF SELF-LOVE .......................................................... 147
KINDNESS AND ACTS OF MERCY ........................................................... 149
COMPASSION FOR OTHERS .................................................................. 151

## CHAPTER 12: DIVINE GUIDANCE AND PERSONAL DISCERNMENT ...... 153

SEEKING GUIDANCE FROM SACRED TEXTS ............................................ 154
PRAYER AS A CHANNEL FOR GUIDANCE ................................................ 156
MEDITATIVE PRACTICES ....................................................................... 158
SPIRITUAL MENTORS AND GUIDES ....................................................... 159

- Scriptural Mentorship .................................................................... 161
- Trusting Intuition and Inner Wisdom ............................................... 163

## CHAPTER 13: RITUALS AND SYMBOLISM AS EXPRESSIONS OF FAITH . 167
- Symbolism in Sacred Objects ........................................................... 167
- Rituals of Initiation and Rites of Passage ......................................... 169
- Healing Rituals and Blessing ........................................................... 171
- Marriage and Wedding Rituals ........................................................ 172
  - *Jewish Marriage Traditions ........................................................ 173*
  - *Christian Marriage Traditions ..................................................... 174*
  - *Islamic Marriage Traditions........................................................ 174*
  - *Differences in Perspective.......................................................... 175*
- Funeral and Mourning Rituals ......................................................... 176
- Pilgrimage and Sacred Journey Rituals ............................................ 177
- Rituals of Repentance and Forgiveness ........................................... 179

## CHAPTER 14: UNITY IN DIVERSITY—EMBRACING DIFFERENCES ......... 183
- Embracing Religious Diversity .......................................................... 184
- Tolerance and Respect .................................................................... 186
- Celebrating Cultural Expressions ..................................................... 188
- Overcoming Religious Prejudice ...................................................... 189
- Interreligious Peacebuilding ............................................................ 191

## CHAPTER 15: CULTIVATING SOULFUL CONNECTIONS ........................ 195
- Nature as a Source of Inspiration .................................................... 197
- Artistic Expression and Creativity .................................................... 200
- Music and Sacred Sounds ................................................................ 202
- Gratitude and Appreciation ............................................................. 205

## CONCLUSION ................................................................................. 209

## AUTHOR'S BIO .............................................................................. 211

## REFERENCES ................................................................................ 213

# Introduction

In the beginning, there was one God! Then, out of this Supreme Being sprung all lifeforms, cultures, religions, deities, and lords.

Like a beautifully entwined vine, the interconnectedness of Judaism, Christianity, and Islam has grown throughout the ages. This divine family tree has resulted in a rich and harmoniously shared heritage and spiritual principles.

These three spiritual paths share a profound bond, tracing their roots back to the legendary figure of Abraham, a patriarch revered by all three faiths. Through the passage of time, their stories have intertwined, bringing together a rich heritage that binds them in kinship.

In the sacred texts of these religions, we find echoes of shared wisdom, moral guidance, and divine revelations. From the Torah to the New Testament and the Quran, each holy scripture is a beacon of light, guiding their communities toward a deeper understanding of life's mysteries.

Moreover, these faiths are united in their belief in one Supreme Being, an omnipotent and benevolent force that transcends all boundaries. This shared monotheistic foundation forms the bedrock of their spiritual endeavors, unifying their spiritual objective for meaning and purpose in a complex, chaotic, and often enigmatic world.

Throughout history, various prophets have graced the lives of these communities, shared divine messages, and exemplified righteous living. Abraham, Moses, Jesus Christ, and the prophet Muhammad are but a few of the luminous figures revered by all three traditions, each leaving an indelible mark on the hearts of their followers.

Ethical principles and concepts of compassion, justice, and kindness resonate deeply within their teachings—urging their adherents to tread a path of righteousness and care for the vulnerable.

However, this embracing of a shared heritage is not without its differences. Diverse interpretations and rituals have given rise to unique expressions of faith, adding to the rich diversity of human spirituality but also stirring up controversy and conflict.

Nonetheless, we find a common thread of hope and redemption in contemplating their eschatological beliefs, envisioning a future where goodness and truth shall triumph over darkness and despair. These visions of a brighter tomorrow instill a sense of purpose and responsibility in their followers to work toward a world of harmony and compassion.

Understanding the interconnectedness of these three faiths fosters a milieu of mutual respect, empathy, and dialogue. As each spiritual path weaves its distinct colors, they create a beautiful mosaic of diversity that enriches our collective understanding of what it means to be human.

In nurturing this bond, we find a shared responsibility to seek common ground, build bridges of cooperation, and stand together in facing the challenges that lie ahead. We can foster a world where love, understanding, and harmony reign supreme by celebrating our shared heritage and spiritual principles.

Throughout the ages, people have sought something more profound, something beyond the tangible: A connection with the Almighty and a greater purpose in life. Religion and spirituality are two fundamental aspects interwoven into the fabric of human existence.

As a result, religion and spirituality have played pivotal roles in shaping individuals' and entire communities' beliefs, values, and practices, spanning cultures and generations.

In essence, religion can be understood as a structured and organized system of beliefs, rituals, and practices, often centered around worshiping one or more deities. It provides a sense of belonging and community, offering solace and guidance to its followers.

In contrast, spirituality is a more personal and inward journey, focusing on self-discovery and seeking a deeper understanding of the universe and one's place. It encourages us to explore our inner selves, values, and connections with the greater cosmos.

The intersection between religion and spirituality is fascinating and complex to explore. Religion provides a framework within which spirituality can be cultivated and flourish—giving structure to personal escapades for spiritual growth and enlightenment.

It offers a support system of like-minded people, providing opportunities for communal worship, shared experiences, and moral guidance.

On the other hand, spirituality delves into individuals' intimate and inner experiences as they seek transformation and enlightenment. It is an odyssey that goes beyond the confines of organized religion and invites us to embark on a personal journey of self-discovery, inner peace, enlightenment, and transcendence.

Spiritual practices come in various forms, from meditation and prayer to yoga and other contemplative activities. These practices serve as tools for self-reflection, mindfulness, and attuning yourself to the spiritual multiverse.

Within the realm of spirituality and religion, the Abrahamic faiths—Judaism, Christianity, and Islam—hold a significant place.

These monotheistic religions share a common origin, tracing their spiritual lineage back to the patriarch Abraham. They all believe in the existence of one God, the Almighty Creator of the universe, and they consider prophets divine messengers who convey God's will.

Abraham holds a significant and revered position in Judaism, Christianity, and Islam. In these Abrahamic religions, he is referred to as a pivotal figure and a prophet, although there are variations in how he is perceived and depicted.

- **Judaism:** In Judaism, Abraham is considered one of the most essential patriarchs and is often called "Avraham Avinu" (Abraham our Father). He is known for his unwavering faith in God and is considered the founder of the Jewish people. According to Jewish tradition, God made a covenant with Abraham, promising him numerous descendants and the land of Canaan as their inheritance. The story of the binding of Isaac (Akedah) is a central event in Judaism, highlighting Abraham's ultimate devotion to God (Libenson, 2021).

- **Christianity:** In Christianity, Abraham is also recognized as a pivotal figure, often referred to as the "Father of Faith" (Libenson, 2021). In the New Testament, he is esteemed as an exemplar of faith and righteousness. The Apostle Paul, in his writings, emphasizes that Abraham's faith in God was counted as righteousness. Christians view Abraham's willingness to sacrifice his son Isaac as a foreshadowing of God's sacrifice of Jesus Christ for the redemption of humanity.

- **Islam:** In Islam, Abraham is honored as a prophet and is referred to as "Ibrahim" in Arabic. He is highly esteemed as one of the major prophets, and his story is recounted in various chapters of the Quran, the holy book of Islam. Muslims believe that Abraham preached monotheism and faced numerous challenges in his mission to spread the message of God's oneness (*Tawheed*). The story of the sacrifice of his son (referred to as Isma'il, or Ishmael, in Islamic tradition) is also recounted in the Quran, where it is emphasized as a test of faith for both Abraham and his son (Stacey, 2023).

- While there are differences in the details and interpretations of Abraham's life and actions among these three religions, his role as a revered prophet and his significance as a central figure in their respective religious narratives highlight the shared heritage and interconnectedness of Judaism, Christianity, and Islam.

- The purpose of delving into these aspects and exploring the significance of religion and spirituality in human life is to acquire knowledge, foster understanding, and promote interfaith dialogue. By acknowledging shared values and recognizing the beauty of diversity within religious traditions, we can bridge gaps and build bridges of respect and cooperation.

Ultimately, religion and spirituality aim to enrich our lives and connection with our Maker and the Earth by cultivating a deeper understanding of ourselves and the various belief systems that shape humanity. Thus, we will be able to find common ground and appreciate the diverse ways in which a person seeks meaning, purpose, and a profound connection with the divine.

**Chapter 1:**

# The Sacred Patriarch Abraham

In the religious traditions of Judaism, Christianity, and Islam, Abraham is central and adored. Widely recognized as the father of monotheism, his influence spans centuries and continues to resonate in the world today. Each faith holds Abraham in high regard, attributing distinct significance to his life and teachings.

In Judaism, Abraham is venerated as the founding father of the unique and sacred relationship between the Jewish people and God. His unwavering faith and obedience to God's call set a profound precedent for future generations, inspiring Jewish believers to cultivate their unique bond with the divine.

Similarly, in Christianity, Abraham's spiritual heritage transcends religious boundaries. He is acknowledged as the spiritual progenitor of all believers, regardless of their background, whether Jewish or non-Jewish. His exemplary life of faith and trust in God is an enduring model for Christians, urging them to nurture a deep connection with the Creator.

In Islam, Abraham occupies a significant position in the lineage of prophets, forming a link that spans from Adam to the final prophet, Muhammad. His devotion to God and his unwavering commitment to monotheism symbolize the essence of Islamic teachings, inspiring Muslims to follow his righteous path (Stacey, 2023).

Abraham's life is a testament to the transformative power of faith, obedience, and trust in God. Despite countless hurdles and trials along the way, he stayed firm in his devotion to the divine vocation. His memory continues to inspire people of faith throughout generations, drawing inspiration from his tenacity and determination.

In a world often marked by divisions, the figure of Abraham serves as a unifying force, binding the three major monotheistic faiths together. His story represents a shared heritage transcending religious boundaries, offering a timeless message of unity, devotion, and righteousness.

Abraham's influence spans millennia, and his story continues to serve as a source of hope and inspiration for people of faith of all theological backgrounds. As we reflect on the life of this extraordinary figure, we are reminded of the enduring power of faith and the potential of unity in embracing common values. Abraham's example serves as a beacon, inspiring us to seek a deeper relationship with the divine and cultivating a sense of spiritual kinship among humanity.

## Abraham's Call and Covenant

The divine summons that called Abraham—previously known as Abram—marked a pivotal moment in his life, as God called him to leave his homeland and journey to an undisclosed land. This sacred call is chronicled in Genesis 12:1–3, where God bestowed upon Abraham the promise of becoming the progenitor of a great nation and being blessed, with all families on Earth finding blessings through him. Despite facing numerous challenges, such as his wife's barrenness and domestic strife, Abraham exhibited unwavering trust in God and dutifully heeded His call (*New International Version,* 2011/1973, Genesis 12:1–3).

The covenant forged between God and Abraham holds enduring significance, comprising three distinct components: the promise of designated land, the assurance of descendants, and the pledge of divine blessings and redemption. This covenant not only marked the genesis of Judaism but also earned Abraham the endearing title of "Avraham Avinu" (Abraham our Father) among the Jewish people (Libenson, 2021).

It signified a momentous shift as Abraham wholeheartedly embraced the one true God and shunned the worship of false deities. The covenant laid the foundation for the unique relationship between God and the Jewish community, which extends through the generations.

Abraham's spiritual journey bore witness to trials and triumphs, yet his unyielding faith in God's promises remained steadfast. His resolute commitment is an exemplary model for humanity, inspiring us to trust God's assurances even amidst seemingly insurmountable circumstances. Abraham's unwavering faith embodied three core virtues: obedience, trust, and fidelity.

His profound expression of faith was demonstrated primarily through his unwavering obedience to God, wherein attentive listening was a prerequisite for understanding and fulfilling the divine will.

As the Father of Faith, Abraham's legacy endures, epitomizing the power of unwavering trust and obedience in God's plans. His story continues to inspire individuals worldwide, igniting the desire to follow in his footsteps of faith, obedience, and trust in God. His enduring impact resonates as a spiritual exemplar for those seeking a life devoted to faith, obedience, and trust in the divine.

# Test of Sacrifice

The Binding of Isaac, a poignant tale from the Hebrew Bible, represents a profound test of Abraham's obedience and unwavering faith. God, as a test of Abraham's devotion, commands him to sacrifice his beloved son, Isaac, on Mount Moriah.

Without hesitation, Abraham sets forth to fulfill God's command, demonstrating his complete trust in divine providence. However, at the crucial moment, an angel intervenes, presenting a ram caught in the thicket as a substitute sacrifice.

Abraham's willingness to follow through with the sacrifice of his son exemplifies a profound surrender to God's will, underlining his unshakable trust in divine wisdom. He believes steadfastly that God will provide for him and his family, even in the face of the most heart-wrenching sacrifice. This submission becomes a test of faith, demanding absolute reliance on God's plan and purpose.

Central to the story, the ram ensnared in the thicket assumes profound symbolism. It serves as a touching reminder of God's intervention at the eleventh hour, sparing Isaac's life and providing an alternative sacrifice. This divine substitution echoes down the ages and finds resonance in the Christian tradition, foreshadowing the ultimate sacrifice of Jesus Christ on the cross.

Throughout history, theologians have offered diverse interpretations of this powerful story. Some view it as a test of Abraham's faith and obedience, while others emphasize the demonstration of God's mercy and love. For some, the Binding of Isaac holds theological significance, paving the way for understanding Christ's redemptive sacrifice.

Contemplating Abraham's willingness to offer his son raises profound ethical questions. Critics argue that blind obedience might overshadow critical moral considerations, while proponents see it as an expression of unwavering trust in God's divine plan. This ancient narrative leaves us pondering the intricacies of sacrifice and the complex interplay between faith and ethics.

The Binding of Isaac remains a timeless tale that challenges our understanding of devotion, sacrifice, and the nature of divine guidance. As we delve into its depths, we encounter a story that transcends time, inviting us to reflect on the profound aspects of the human-spiritual relationship.

## Father of Nations

Abraham's profound influence on the world is attested by his title as the Father of Nations, and his multicultural legacy is a testament to this fact. All three Abrahamic faiths, Christianity, Judaism, and Islam, recognize him as their common forefather.

A significant aspect of Abraham's legacy is fulfilling divine promises regarding his descendants. Through his sons Isaac and Ishmael and subsequent generations, God's covenant with Abraham ensured that he would be the father of many nations and that kings would arise from his bloodline.

The blessings and promises bestowed upon Abraham's descendants are also integral to his legacy. God assured his progeny of designated land, the land of Canaan, and expanded this promise to encompass all the territory within his sight. As detailed in Genesis 17, the covenant established an everlasting commitment from God to grant the land of Canaan to

Abraham's descendants in perpetuity (*New International Version,* 2011/1973, Genesis 17).

Moreover, the shared ancestry among the Abrahamic faiths underscores the interconnectedness of their spiritual heritage. Jews, Christians, and Muslims draw upon their sacred texts to trace their history back to Abraham and explore the evolved interpretations.

The diversity of interpretations and practices within the Abrahamic faiths further enriches his legacy. Varied Jewish, Christian, and Muslim traditions concerning Abraham reflect their communities' multifaceted beliefs and customs throughout different times and regions.

Abraham's enduring legacy lies not only in his role as the Father of Nations but also in his profound impact on the shared heritage of the Abrahamic faiths. Through the fulfillment of divine promises and unity amid diversity, his legacy inspires believers across generations and cultures.

## Abraham's Journey and Migrations

Abraham's story commences in the ancient and bustling city of Ur, situated in the fertile region of Mesopotamia. Mesopotamia, known as the "land between rivers," was a cradle of civilization, flourishing with advanced cultures, innovations, and trade. It was amidst this vibrant backdrop that Abraham's journey of faith and obedience began.

## *Origin in Ur of the Chaldeans*

The turning point in Abraham's life came with God's divine call, a momentous and life-altering event. In response to this call, Abraham embarked on a profound and transformative journey, leaving behind the comforts and familiarity of his homeland to venture into the unknown. God's calling was not merely a physical relocation but a spiritual call to a higher purpose and destiny.

As Abraham set forth on this journey, he needed to understand its ultimate destination completely. God led him to a land that was yet undisclosed, and it was through faith and trust in God's guidance that he embarked on this sacred pilgrimage. This journey embodied his dedication to follow God's will, even when the path ahead remained obscured.

The foundation of Abraham's journey lay in his unwavering obedience to God's commands. He demonstrated a profound devotion and trust, never hesitating to respond to God's call. Abraham's faithfulness was deeply rooted in the promises and covenant God had made with him. God assured Abraham that his descendants would inherit this chosen land, a divine promise that would shape the destiny of countless generations.

Abraham's obedience was not driven by blind compliance but by an unwavering faith in God's promises. His belief in fulfilling God's covenant fueled his determination to continue this journey, even when faced with challenges and uncertainties.

Abraham's story is a testament to the power of faith and the transformative nature of obedience. It exemplifies a profound trust in a higher purpose, even when the path seems uncertain or arduous. His unwavering dedication to following God's call established a legacy that resonates through the ages.

## *Journey to Canaan*

Abraham's journey to Canaan was a remarkable and eventful expedition, filled with trials and divine encounters. After leaving his homeland of Ur in Mesopotamia, Abraham and his father Terah and their families settled in Haran. Haran, situated along the ancient trade routes, provided a prosperous and stable environment for them to reside.

During their time in Haran, Abraham experienced the loss of his father, Terah, who lived to age 205. The passing of a loved one is always a significant event, and it likely presented Abraham with a moment of reflection and introspection. Little is mentioned in the scriptures about their stay in Haran, leaving the reason for their temporary settlement open to speculation.

During this time of transition and loss, God called Abraham again, instructing him to resume the journey to Canaan. This divine call was a pivotal moment in Abraham's life, reaffirming his purpose and destiny as the progenitor of a great nation. God's command required Abraham to uproot his family once more and set forth on a path with an unknown destination.

Leaving behind the comfort and familiarity of Haran must have been a daunting decision, but it was a testament to Abraham's immense faith and trust in God's plan. The journey to Canaan was not just a physical relocation but a spiritual and transformative pilgrimage guided by divine providence.

Abraham's unwavering faith in God's call enabled him to face the challenges and uncertainties ahead. It required deep trust in the unseen and a steadfast commitment to follow divine guidance, even when the journey seemed complex or unclear. Abraham's journey to Canaan is a powerful reminder of the courage and conviction that come with a life dedicated to faith and obedience to a higher purpose.

## *Sojourn in Egypt*

Amidst a severe famine gripping the land, Abraham faced the pressing need to seek refuge in Egypt. The scarcity of food and resources made survival in the region a formidable challenge, prompting him to consider alternative options to ensure the well-being of his family.

As they approached Egypt, Abraham faced a unique dilemma. His wife Sarai was renowned for her beauty, and he knew that her striking appearance might draw unwanted attention from the Egyptians. Fearing for her safety and their welfare, Abraham took precautionary measures to protect Sarai and himself in this unfamiliar territory.

To safeguard their well-being, Abraham devised a plan. He instructed Sarai to identify herself as his sister rather than his wife, believing that this would avert potential threats. In doing so, he sought to mitigate the risks they might face as foreigners in a land without familial ties or protection.

This temporary sojourn in Egypt allowed Abraham and his family to endure the challenges of the famine. While they found temporary relief from the scarcity of food and resources, it was a time of profound vulnerability and uncertainty. The decision to venture into Egypt was not without its ethical complexities, and it highlighted the lengths to which one might go to ensure survival in times of hardship.

Despite the pragmatic approach taken by Abraham, the story of his time in Egypt reminds us of the complexities of human decision-making and the moral dilemmas that arise in challenging circumstances. It also demonstrates Abraham's depths of concern and caring for his family's safety and well-being.

The narrative serves as a potent reminder that even in moments of hardship and desperation, individuals must grapple with ethical considerations and the potential consequences of their actions. Abraham's time in Egypt exemplifies the complexities of human existence, where survival and moral choices intersect in a manner that tests one's principles and values.

Ultimately, the story of Abraham's journey to Egypt highlights the human struggle to balance practicality and morality, especially in the face of adversity. It also underscores the importance of making decisions that align with one's principles and beliefs, even when navigating uncertain and challenging circumstances.

## *Wells, Altars, and Nomadic Life*

Abraham established wells and altars throughout his journey, each bearing profound significance. Altars symbolized worship and offering to God, a place of sacrifice and connection with the divine. Wells held both practical and symbolic importance, providing sustenance for his family and flocks while serving as markers of territorial ownership.

Embracing a nomadic lifestyle, Abraham and his descendants led a pastoral existence, tending to their flocks of sheep, goats, and other animals. These herds provided essential resources such as milk, meat, wool, and leather, while donkeys and camels aided in transporting goods and facilitating long-range travel. This nomadic way of life demanded various skills, from grazing and watering the animals to protecting them from predators and locating strays.

Abraham's journey and migrations signify a physical passage from one place to another and a profound spiritual odyssey guided by unwavering faith in God's providence. His story is one of countless challenges, encounters, and acts of devotion, exemplifying the strength of trust and obedience in a divine plan that transcends time and space.

## Abraham's Relationship With God

A unique and covenantal friendship characterized Abraham's relationship with God. God entered into a solemn covenant with Abraham, promising to make him the father of many nations and to bestow upon him and his descendants the land of Canaan as an everlasting possession. This covenant formed the bedrock of their special bond, uniting them in a profound and enduring connection.

Central to their relationship were the divine promises made by God to Abraham. God pledged to bless Abraham and transform him into a great nation, with his descendants becoming a source of blessing for all families on Earth. These promises served as a guiding force, shaping their mutual trust and deepening their intimacy.

Abraham's compassion for others and his longing for justice were evident in his intercession for the cities of Sodom and Gomorrah. When he learned of God's plans to destroy these cities, Abraham pleaded for their salvation, demonstrating his empathy for their inhabitants and unwavering commitment to righteousness.

Hospitality was a significant aspect of Abraham's character and played a vital role in inviting divine encounters. On one occasion, Abraham's warm welcome of three strangers led to a momentous revelation as these strangers turned out to be angels sent by God. This divine visitation underscored the importance of hospitality and highlighted the profound connection between Abraham and the divine.

Abraham's righteousness was intricately tied to his faith in God. The Bible records that his faith was counted as righteousness in the eyes of God. This exemplifies the transformative power of faith, for Abraham's righteousness was credited to him through his unwavering belief in God's promises.

Abraham's relationship with God is a timeless example of the beauty of covenantal friendship, anchored in trust, compassion, and faith. Their story resonates through the ages, inspiring countless believers to seek a profound and intimate connection with the divine. As we reflect on their extraordinary bond, we are reminded of faith's transformative power, righteousness's significance, and the profound impact of hospitality and intercession in our spiritual journeys.

## Key Takeaways

Abraham's pivotal divine call and his unwavering response set the stage for a covenantal relationship with God. God called Abraham to leave his homeland and journey to a new land, and in return, promised to make him the father of many nations and bless all families on Earth through him. This covenant marked the beginning of Judaism and shaped Abraham's role as the founding father of a special relationship between the Jewish people and God.

The poignant story of the "Binding of Isaac," a test of Abraham's faith and obedience, showcases his profound devotion to God. In this challenge, God instructs Abraham to kill his beloved son, Isaac. Abraham's willingness to fulfill God's command exemplifies an actual test of faith and surrender to divine providence. Ultimately, God intervenes, providing a ram as a substitute sacrifice, highlighting the importance of trust in God's plan and mercy.

Abraham's legacy as the Father of Nations is a testament to his enduring impact on the world. Recognized by Judaism, Christianity, and Islam as their common forefather, Abraham's influence extends across religious boundaries. His fulfillment of divine promises, blessings, and shared ancestry among the Abrahamic faiths symbolize unity amid diversity, inspiring people of faith worldwide.

Abraham's journey from Ur of the Chaldeans to Canaan, with stops in Haran and Egypt, epitomizes a profound spiritual odyssey. His obedience and nomadic lifestyle demonstrate his unwavering trust in God's providence. Abraham's encounters with various challenges, wells, and altars reflect his resilience and devotion to God's plan.

Abraham's covenantal friendship with God is a timeless example of devotion and unity. His unwavering faith, compassion, hospitality, and righteousness epitomize the profound connection between a believer and the divine. Abraham's story unites the three major monotheistic faiths, emphasizing the transformative power of faith, trust, and obedience in shaping a profound spiritual journey.

This chapter highlighted Abraham's profound influence and enduring legacy across the religious traditions of Judaism, Christianity, and Islam. Abraham's life exemplifies faith, obedience, and trust in God, inspiring believers of all backgrounds to seek a deeper spiritual connection and cultivate unity amid diverse religious expressions.

## Chapter 2:

# One God, Many Paths

The belief in one God, central to Judaism, Christianity, and Islam, serves as a foundational pillar that profoundly shapes the spiritual paths of these religions. It provides a unifying framework for believers to understand their relationship with the divine, influencing their personal and communal practices.

One of the significant aspects of monotheism is its emphasis on a personal and intimate connection between God and us. In each of these faiths, followers can establish a direct and meaningful relationship with the one God through prayer, worship, and other spiritual practices. This personal connection fosters a sense of closeness and devotion, strengthening our faith and commitment to our religious path.

Furthermore, monotheism suggests that there is one ultimate source of truth and morality. This belief in an all-knowing and all-powerful God lays the foundation for ethical conduct, providing a moral compass that guides believers in their actions and decision-making. The belief in the singular divine authority establishes a coherent moral framework that informs the ethical principles and values upheld by each religion.

The concept of monotheism also underscores the interconnectedness of all Creation. Believers in one God recognize that everything in the universe is subject to the divine will, creating a sense of unity and purpose in the world. This interconnectedness extends to humanity and the natural world, encouraging believers to view themselves as stewards of the

Earth and being responsible for preserving its beauty and diversity.

The belief in one God profoundly shapes how we perceive our place in the world and our relationships with others. It fosters a sense of humility and reverence for the divine, acknowledging human limitations in understanding the vastness of God's wisdom and plan. This recognition of the divine's ultimate sovereignty encourages us to approach life with a sense of purpose and devotion.

The belief in one God is a central and unifying tenet of the Abrahamic religions. It informs the personal relationship between humans and God, guides ethical conduct, and emphasizes the interconnectedness of all Creation. This belief serves as a guiding light for believers, providing a sense of purpose, moral guidance, and spiritual fulfillment in their respective faiths.

## Monotheism as the Core Belief

Monotheism—the belief in one God—stands as a fundamental and unifying tenet that binds the Abrahamic traditions of Judaism, Christianity, and Islam together (van Baaren, 2023). This core belief serves as the backbone of their spiritual ideologies and is the pivotal point from which their shared heritage emanates.

In contrast to polytheistic belief systems that venerate multiple gods or deities, monotheism holds that there is only one supreme and all-encompassing God. While polytheistic religions often ascribe different gods to specific domains or aspects of life, monotheistic religions emphasize the singular, all-powerful nature of the divine.

The theological implications of monotheism are profound. The belief in one God suggests a unifying force that underpins all of creation, implying an interconnectedness and purpose to existence. This singular source of truth and morality becomes the foundation upon which the ethical and spiritual principles of these religions are built.

The concept of monotheism shapes personal spiritual experiences by providing us with a framework to understand our relationship with the Almighty. In monotheistic traditions, we can engage in a personal and direct connection with God through prayer, worship, and other spiritual practices. This intimate bond with the one God serves as a source of guidance, comfort, and inspiration for followers.

Despite the diversity of interpretations and practices within the Abrahamic traditions, monotheism serves as a unifying force, creating a sense of commonality among Jews, Christians, and Muslims. It forms a shared foundation upon which their spiritual beliefs and practices are built, fostering a sense of spiritual kinship among believers.

The concept of monotheism has shaped the history, culture, and values of these religions, leaving an indelible mark on the course of human civilization. Through their shared belief in one God, Jews, Christians, and Muslims find a common thread that ties them together.

As the core belief that transcends time and geographical boundaries, monotheism represents a testament to the enduring power of faith in a singular divine presence. It continues to inspire believers across generations, encouraging us to seek spiritual fulfillment and understanding in the embrace of the one God who unifies all of humanity.

# Conceptions of God

Conceptions of God in the Abrahamic traditions encompass a complex and multifaceted understanding of the God of Creation. While the specifics may vary among Judaism, Christianity, and Islam, there are overarching themes that unite their perspectives on God.

- **Attributes of God:** One of the central aspects of monotheistic conceptions of God is the belief in divine attributes. God is often described as all-knowing (omniscient), all-powerful (omnipotent), and all-present (omnipresent). These attributes emphasize God's supreme and limitless nature, underscoring the idea that God is beyond human comprehension.

- **Personal and transcendent:** The perception of God as both personal and transcendent gives rise to a profound tension in understanding the Creator. On the one hand, God is seen as intimately involved in the lives of believers, capable of forming a personal relationship with us through prayer and devotion. On the other hand, God is transcendent, existing beyond the limits of the material world and human understanding.

- **Names and titles of God:** The diverse names, titles, and metaphors used to refer to God reflect the richness of the Abrahamic traditions. Each tradition has its unique ways of addressing and understanding the Highest. For example, in Judaism, God is often referred to as Yahweh or Adonai, while in Islam, God is called Allah, and in Christianity, God is addressed as Father, Son (Jesus Christ), and Holy Spirit (the Trinity).

- **God's relationship with Creation:** All three traditions share the belief in God as the Creator of the universe and everything within it. This understanding has profound implications for humans as stewards of Creation. It instills a sense of responsibility for caring for the Earth and its inhabitants, recognizing that all of Creation is interconnected and interdependent.

- **Mystery and incomprehensibility:** Monotheistic conceptions of God acknowledge the mystery and incomprehensibility of the divine. While believers may seek to deepen their understanding of God through prayer, study, and reflection, they recognize that God's true nature remains beyond human grasp. This recognition of the divine mystery humbles us and fosters a sense of awe and reverence toward God (van Baaren, 2023).

Conceptions of God in the Abrahamic traditions embrace the belief in a singular, all-powerful, and all-knowing Creator who is both personal and transcendent. The diverse names, titles, and metaphors used to refer to God highlight the richness of each tradition's understanding.

The relationship between God and Creation shapes the ethical and moral perspectives of believers, inspiring us to act as responsible stewards of the world. Amidst the mystery and incomprehensibility of the Almighty, the concept of God unites Jews, Christians, and Muslims in our shared belief in the one true God.

# Creation of the Universe and Humanity

Divine Creation in the Abrahamic traditions is a fundamental belief that unites Judaism, Christianity, and Islam. This shared belief holds that God is the Creator of the universe, and all that exists is a product of His divine will and creative power. The act of Creation is often seen as an expression of divine love, reflecting God's goodness, beauty, and desire to share His Creation with all beings (Haarsma, 2018).

The concept of Creation as an act of love emphasizes the benevolent nature of God. By bringing the world into existence, God bestows the gift of life upon His Creation, demonstrating His love and care for all living beings. This act of love is not limited to any specific group or person but extends universally, embracing the entire created order.

The Abrahamic faiths view humans as bearers of the divine image, endowing them with inherent dignity and worth. This belief underlines the equality and intrinsic value of all human beings, regardless of their background, ethnicity, or social status. Recognizing the divine image in each person emphasizes the importance of treating others with respect, compassion, and kindness.

As stewards of Creation, humans are entrusted with the responsibility to care for the natural world and its resources. This role as caretakers reflects the belief that God has made humanity co-creators, entrusting us with the task of preserving the beauty and diversity of the environment. This responsibility is grounded in the understanding that the Earth and its resources are not limitless and should be used thoughtfully and sustainably.

The belief in a purpose and destiny for humanity is central to the Abrahamic traditions. Each believer is seen as having a unique role to play in God's grand plan for the universe. This belief imbues human lives with meaning, emphasizing that our actions and choices have significance within the larger context of God's divine purpose. It encourages people to seek purposeful lives that align with God's will and contribute positively to the well-being of others and the world.

The concept of divine Creation in the Abrahamic traditions reflects the belief in a loving and benevolent God who created the universe out of love and goodness. This belief bestows upon humans inherent dignity and worth, making us responsible stewards of Creation. Embracing the notion of a purposeful destiny, believers are encouraged to lead meaningful lives in harmony with God's plan and to demonstrate love and care for all of God's Creation.

## Divine Revelation and Transcendence

In the Abrahamic religions, divine revelation is a central concept, and it is believed to come through sacred texts that are considered the word of God. These texts, such as the Torah in Judaism, the Bible in Christianity, and the Quran in Islam, are regarded as repositories of divine knowledge and guidance for humanity. They are considered to be the culmination of God's communication with humanity through prophets and other intermediaries (Wahlberg, 2020).

Prophets hold a significant role in the Abrahamic religions as messengers of God. They are chosen by God to deliver His revelations and guidance to the people. These prophets act as intermediaries, bridging the gap between the Most High and the human race, and their messages are considered divinely inspired.

The transmission of divine revelation is often through both oral and written traditions. In ancient times, before the advent of writing, revelations were orally transmitted by the prophets and memorized by their followers. Subsequently, these revelations were recorded in written form to ensure their preservation and widespread dissemination.

Miracles are considered manifestations of divine power in the Abrahamic religions. They serve as signs of God's presence and intervention in the world and are often associated with the work of prophets and other holy figures. Miracles are believed to be supernatural events that defy natural laws and provide evidence of God's divine authority and involvement in human affairs.

Despite the revelations and miracles experienced by believers, there is an acknowledgment of the transcendence and mystery of God. The divine nature is ultimately beyond human comprehension, and despite the revelations, there remains an element of mystery and awe surrounding God's essence. The recognition of God's transcendence highlights the humility and reverence with which believers approach God.

Divine revelation is a pivotal aspect of the Abrahamic religions, conveyed through sacred texts and delivered by prophets. These texts are considered the word of God, providing guidance, laws, and wisdom to believers. Miracles serve as divine manifestations of power and presence.

However, amidst these revelations and miracles, there is a profound recognition of God's transcendence and the inherent mystery that surrounds the divine nature. This understanding fosters humility and reverence in the face of the Almighty's incomprehensible greatness.

# Morality and Worship

Monotheism is a fundamental belief that unites the Abrahamic traditions of Judaism, Christianity, and Islam. It stands in stark contrast to polytheistic belief systems, which advocate the worship of multiple gods or deities, each associated with specific aspects of nature or human experience. In contrast, monotheistic religions affirm the existence of only one all-powerful and all-knowing God (Beyer, 2018).

The significance of monotheism is profound, as it implies the presence of a single, ultimate source of truth and morality. This belief posits that there is a cohesive and interconnected nature to all of Creation, and everything is subject to the will of the Most High God. This unity in the divine nature fosters a sense of purpose and order in the universe.

One of the theological implications of monotheism is the concept of divine providence. Believers in a singular God recognize that all events and circumstances are under His control and that there is a divine plan for every individual and the world as a whole. This understanding can bring comfort and reassurance in times of uncertainty, knowing that everything is guided by the wisdom of the one God.

Furthermore, monotheism shapes personal spiritual experiences by providing a framework for understanding the relationship between God and us. In monotheistic religions, believers can establish a personal connection with God through prayer, worship, and other spiritual practices. This direct relationship with the Divine fosters a sense of intimacy and closeness, enhancing our faith and commitment to the teachings of our faith.

Despite the diversity of interpretations and practices within the Abrahamic traditions, monotheism serves as a unifying force. It provides a common foundation for believers across these religions, underscoring our shared belief in the one God. This unifying element encourages mutual respect and understanding among the followers of Judaism, Christianity, and Islam.

Monotheism is a core belief that unifies the Abrahamic traditions. It emphasizes the existence of one all-powerful God, distinct from polytheistic belief systems. The theological implications of monotheism underscore the interconnectedness of all Creation and the existence of a single source of truth and morality. This belief shapes personal spiritual experiences and provides a unifying framework within the diverse landscape of the Abrahamic religions.

## Key Takeaways

Monotheism unifies the Abrahamic traditions (Judaism, Christianity, and Islam) with the belief in one God, in contrast to polytheistic belief systems. Theological implications of monotheism include recognizing a single, ultimate source of truth and morality and the interconnectedness of all Creation.

Attributes of God in the Abrahamic traditions reflect His characteristics and nature. The tension in perceiving God as both personal and transcendent emphasizes His immanence and transcendence. Different names, titles, and metaphors are used to refer to God, enriching the understanding of His divine nature.

God's relationship with Creation as the Creator implies human responsibility as stewards of the natural world. The mystery and incomprehensibility inherent in monotheistic conceptions of God acknowledge the limitations of human understanding. The belief in God as the Creator of the universe and humanity reflects an expression of divine love and goodness.

Humans are considered bearers of the divine image, deserving of inherent dignity and worth. As stewards of Creation, humans have a responsibility to care for and protect the natural world. The belief in a purpose and destiny for humanity underscores the significance of individual lives in God's larger plan.

Divine revelation comes through sacred texts, prophets, and miracles, serving as manifestations of God's presence and power. Prophets act as messengers, delivering divine guidance to humanity. Both oral and written traditions play a role in transmitting and preserving divine revelation.

The mysterious nature of divine revelation acknowledges God's transcendence and incomprehensibility. The belief in one God provides a moral framework and ethical principles that guide believers' conduct.

Worship is seen as an expression of devotion, allowing for personal spiritual experiences and connection with God. Ethical monotheism links faith to ethical conduct and righteous behavior. Prayer and supplication are essential in seeking guidance, support, and a deeper connection with God.

Virtues and character development are cultivated within monotheistic faiths, guiding believers in living virtuous lives aligned with their beliefs.

This chapter highlighted the central tenets and beliefs that shape the Abrahamic traditions, emphasizing monotheism, the nature of God, divine revelation, human responsibility, and the importance of ethical conduct and worship.

Chapter 3:

# Sacred Texts—Torah, Bible, and Quran

At the heart of the sacred texts, the Quran, Bible, and Torah, lies a profound belief in their divine authorship. This belief serves as a cornerstone of faith and guides humanity through their respective teachings and revelations.

## The Torah

The traditional view of Judaism is that God revealed the Torah to Moses, either through direct speech or inspiration, along with the Oral Torah. However, there is no consensus among the rabbis on when and how the whole Torah was given to the Jewish people. Some believe that the entire Torah was revealed at once on Mount Sinai, where Orthodox rabbis date Moses' encounter with God to 1280 B.C.E. According to this view, every word in the Torah, even those that describe Moses' death and what happened after, came from God's mouth (*Torah*, n.d.).

Others argue that the Torah was revealed gradually over many years, until Moses' death. Some also suggest that some parts of the Torah were written by another prophet after Moses, such as

Joshua. They point out that some verses contain information that was not known during Moses' lifetime (*Torah*, n.d.).

However, not all rabbis agree with this idea. Modern scholars propose a different theory, called the Documentary Hypothesis, which claims that the Torah has multiple authors (*Torah*, n.d.). They trace the development of the text over more than a thousand years, from ancient poems and songs to an Israelite epic from King Solomon's time, to different versions from the Northern and Southern kingdoms, to a seventh-century edition of Deuteronomy, to priestly sources.

They believe that these sources were combined over time until the final form of the Torah was established in the time of Ezra the Scribe. The Talmud also mentions a special section in Numbers, which is marked by inverted Hebrew letter nuns. It says that this section forms a separate book. A midrash on Proverbs says that this section comes from a hidden book. Another midrash, Ta'ame Haserot Viyterot, links this section to the prophecy of Eldad and Medad (*Torah*, n.d.).

The Talmud also says that God dictated four books of the Torah to Moses, but Moses wrote Deuteronomy in his own words. Despite these discussions, classical views affirm that the Torah is mostly from Moses and God.

## The Bible

The Bible reveals God's intentions, His creative acts, His desires for humanity, His historical plan, and His salvation through Jesus Christ. It conveys its content propositionally and is comprehended and embraced by those illuminated by the Holy Spirit.

"The Bible is a collection of sixty six books written by nearly forty human authors spanning approximately sixteen hundred years" (Cook, 2017). These works came to life, with the original manuscripts written in Hebrew and Koine Greek, while certain sections were recorded in Aramaic, as highlighted in Cook's research (2017). It's intriguing to note that behind each human writer, there exists a Divine author, guiding and inspiring their writings. This Divine influence shaped the Bible into a document that not only conveys the thoughts and messages of these writers but also serves as a revelation of God's intentions, His magnificent acts of creation, His profound desires for humanity, His unfolding historical plan, and the pathway to salvation through Jesus Christ.

It conveys its content propositionally and is comprehended and embraced by those illuminated by the Holy Spirit. The Bible's inspiration originates from the Divine. Although, the way people perceive the idea of being inspired is never the same, the concept of "verbal plenary inspiration" most closely aligns with the Bible's self-portrayals (Cook, 2017). As Cook (2017) noted, this type of inspiration asserts that God is the divine author of the Bible, which includes His very words across the entirety of the text. The Apostle Paul claimed that his writings were written by the Divine Author, emphasizing that the Thessalonian Christians accepted them as such (Cook, 2017).

Numerous English translations accurately depict the original meaning of divinely inspired writers. Most individuals read the word of God, much like any other literary work. Although certain passages present challenges, a significant portion of the Bible is readily understandable.

In essence, the Scripture is a history book, illustrating God's interactions with individuals. Additionally, it also encompasses various genres, including "law, prophecy, Psalms, proverbs, poetry, parables, and epistles" (Cook, 2017). A literal interpretation is crucial for discerning the author's intent in these genres and avoiding fanciful interpretations that deviate from the text's plain meaning.

Despite advocating for a nonliteral reading of the Bible, proponents of this approach expect their own words to be taken literally. To maintain objectivity, a straightforward interpretation is essential. The following guideline prevents unwarranted speculation (Cook, 2017):

> When the plain sense of Scripture makes common sense, seek no other sense; therefore, take every word at its primary, ordinary, usual, and literal meaning unless the facts of the immediate context, studied in the light of related passages and axiomatic and fundamental truths, clearly indicate otherwise. (para. 5)

The "grammatical-historical method of interpretation" is crucial for a normative understanding of God's Word (Cook, 2017). This method calls for a comprehensive grasp of God's Word, involving strict adherence to grammatical rules and an exploration of the historical significance of words. It demands meticulous examination of every word and verse within both their immediate context and the larger context of the book and the entirety of God's Word.

The Bible remains God's written revelation, which has stood the test of time, depicting His identity and accomplishments throughout history. A plain and literal interpretation, grounded in the grammatical-historical method, best captures the Bible's intended message as conveyed through its human writers under the divine guidance of the Holy Spirit.

# The Quran

Just as with any religious scripture, the Quran holds a significant place in understanding Islam, both in its present practice and its historical origins. Since many non-Muslims haven't read the Quran, it's important to provide a brief overview. The term *Quran* means "recitation" in Arabic and is thought to be derived from the Syriac word "Quryana," referring to liturgical readings (*Quran: Divine authorship or authored by men?* 2019). According to this source, as the sacred Islamic text, the Quran serves as a primary "source of guidance for Muslims," though much of Islamic law (*Sharia*) is drawn from other sources like the *Hadith* (sayings of Muhammad), the *Sira* (biography of Muhammad), *Tafsir* (Quranic commentary), and *Fiqh* (Islamic jurisprudence).

Comprising 114 chapters or *Surahs*, the Quran offers teachings on various subjects, including Allah's greatness, relations with Jews and Christians, interactions with non-Muslims, and Muslim conduct in prayer, charity, marriage, and conflicts. Unlike Christian or Jewish scriptures, the Quran's organization is based on chapter length rather than chronology. It also contains stories of Old Testament figures (Moses, David, and Abraham) and narratives about Jesus (referred to as "Isa") and his mother, Mary (*Quran: Divine authorship or authored by men?* 2019).

## *The Traditional Muslim Perspective*

The Quran is paramount to Muslims, serving as a foundational text that shapes their understanding of God and instructs their interactions with others. Several key aspects shed light on the nature of the Quran. Muslims assert that the Quran is the most perfect book ever revealed, transmitted to Muhammad by the angel Gabriel, and then documented shortly after Muhammad's death. This version is believed to be the same as the one existing today. As the final divine revelation, Muslims contend that the Quran corrects and supersedes previous scriptures, including the Bible, which they claim has been altered by humans.

Central to the Islamic faith is Muhammad's direct experience in receiving the Quran. He received revelations from Gabriel over a span of 23 years, beginning in 610 and continuing until his death in 632. Unlike the Bible, which is seen as inspired by God and written by humans, the Quran is regarded as a word-by-word dictation to Muhammad, a direct message from God. Although Muhammad couldn't read or write, he received revelations in a cave near Mecca, memorized them, and recited them to the people.

Following his death, his successors realized the need to compile these oral recitations into a written book to preserve the exact wording. Portions of the Quran were written down on various materials and collected during the time of Uthman (approximately 650 A.D.), the third Caliph, to create a unified version. This compilation was then distributed to Islamic centers of influence (*Quran: Divine authorship or authored by men?* 2019).

## *Supporting the Quran's Authenticity*

Muslims offer various reasons to validate the Quran's authenticity. First, they highlight verses within the Quran itself that emphasize the gradual, perfect, and preserved nature of the revelation. These verses demonstrate the divine origin of the Quran. Second, Muslims believe that the original Quran is eternally preserved in heaven. This belief underscores the sacredness of the text and its divine origin. Additionally,

Muslims assert that the Quran is the final revelation, intended to correct and confirm earlier scriptures.

The meticulous writing process further reinforces the Quran's authenticity. Although the Quran was finalized years after Muhammad's death, Muslims view Uthman's compilation as a faithful representation of the eternal revelation. While some verses were recorded during Muhammad's lifetime, the majority were documented after his death. Uthman's collection aimed to preserve the exact words of Muhammad by gathering oral testimonies and written fragments. Muslims believe that this version, completed around 650 A.D., accurately reflects the words of Allah (*Quran: Divine authorship or authored by men?* 2019).

The Quran's language and aesthetic appeal serve as additional evidence of its authenticity. The text's literary beauty and eloquence are viewed as signs of divine authorship. Muhammad defended the divine nature of the Quran based on its unparalleled literary style and challenged unbelievers to produce anything comparable.

Consequently, Muslims firmly believe in the Quran's divine origin, based on its internal evidence, compilation process, and literary excellence. This belief forms the foundation for their conviction in its superiority over other scriptures and its role as the final revelation.

## Core Teachings and Moral Values

Within the intricate weave of religious traditions, core teachings, and moral values serve as guiding beacons for believers' ethical conduct and spiritual growth. This exploration explores the ethical teachings and moral values central to Judaism, Christianity, and Islam.

Judaism's moral compass is rooted in the Torah, a timeless guide that shapes the lives of its adherents. On the other hand, Christianity finds its moral bedrock in the Bible, championing values that starkly contrast with worldly desires.

Meanwhile, the teachings of the Prophet Muhammad crystallize the essence of Islam, encapsulating beliefs and practices that foster devotion, compassion, and harmony. The central ethical principles of each tradition weave an elaborate composition of values that illuminate the path toward righteousness and meaningful existence (*Quran: Divine authorship or authored by men?* 2019).

## *Ethical Teachings of Judaism*

In Judaism, moral and ethical principles find their roots in the Torah, a foundational guide for living. Learning and imparting Torah knowledge is emphasized as a crucial directive (Sharma, 2022).

Halachah, the legal dimension of Judaism, steers followers toward a harmonious relationship with God and fellow humans. It delves into the intricacies of ethical Jewish living, elaborating on the guidelines outlined in the Torah's 613 mitzvot (commandments), which are further illuminated within the Talmud.

Ethical guidance for Jewish individuals is deeply rooted in the Torah, encompassing both the written and oral Torah (Talmud). These 613 mitzvot can be categorized as positive actions and negative abstentions. The Ten Commandments encapsulate these commandments, focusing on the connection between God and the people of Israel and interpersonal interactions.

Prophets, chosen by a divine call, bravely conveyed messages to their communities, challenging authority and advocating for social reform grounded in Torah principles. Often met with resistance, these prophets upheld ideals of equality, justice, and peace, embodying the essence of *tikkun olam*—the mending of the world.

*Tikkun olam*, meaning "restoration of the world," signifies Judaism's commitment to social justice in partnership with the divine (Sharma, 2022). This concept recognizes the significance of individual contributions in pursuing a state of harmony and wholeness.

Tzedakah, an integral part of *tikkun olam*, accentuates acts of charity and generosity within reasonable bounds, without endangering one's own well-being. This principle not only emphasizes the act of giving but also outlines acceptable ways of giving, aligning with Catholic Social Teaching's concept of prioritizing the well-being of the disadvantaged.

*Gemilut Chasidim*, encompassed by *tikkun olam*, involves compassionate acts such as visiting the sick, comforting mourners, or offering hospitality. *Bal tashchit*, in contrast, discourages the needless destruction of nature, fostering an ethos of responsible environmental stewardship.

The Book of Proverbs, attributed to King Solomon, imparts practical wisdom and underscores the value of Torah study. It encourages cultivating positive attributes such as wisdom, righteousness, purity, and a generous spirit, all resonating with ethical principles.

In essence, these teachings underscore Judaism's unwavering commitment to ethical conduct, social equity, ecological responsibility, and the pursuit of wisdom, all firmly rooted in the diligent study and application of the Torah.

## *Christian Values and Christian Life*

Worldly values encompass desires for wealth, power, pleasure, revenge, fame, vanity, and status. These desires are paramount for individuals who perceive no higher purpose beyond themselves. Such values often breed envy, resentment, and conflicts, aligning with the intentions of malevolent forces.

In contrast, the values espoused by the Bible frequently stand in opposition to worldly ideals. These biblical principles prioritize kindness and respect for all, replacing power, humility over status, honesty and generosity above wealth, self-control rather than self-indulgence, and forgiveness in lieu of revenge.

Christian values promote harmony and goodwill among people in alignment with divine intentions. Although attaining perfection in life is an elusive goal, those who earnestly follow God's commandments often discover a sense of joy and peace that transcends material rewards.

Outlined below are ten values or principles underscored prominently in the Bible (*What does the Bible,* n.d.):

1. **Devotion to God alone:** Jesus, when asked about the greatest commandment, emphasized the supreme importance of loving God wholeheartedly. The Bible warns against replacing our devotion to God with idols or false gods, recognizing that anything overshadowing this devotion is a breach of the first commandment. Jesus particularly warned against the allure of wealth as a competing idol.

In contemporary times, various distractions lock horns for our devotion, such as excessive focus on material possessions, pursuit of wealth, power, fame, or pleasure, and undue attachment to self, work, ideologies, or even family.

2. **Compassion for all:** Following the affirmation of love for God, Jesus emphasized the command to love one's neighbor as oneself. This love, represented by the Greek term "agape," encompasses respect, benevolence, goodwill, and genuine concern for others' well-being.

   The parable of the Good Samaritan illustrates the universal application of Christian love to all individuals, transcending divisions of race, religion, and nationality. Moreover, Christians are encouraged to extend this love even to their adversaries.

3. **Embracing humility:** Humility involves showing respectful consideration for others and contrasts arrogance, boastfulness, and vanity. Humble behavior acknowledges the inherent worth of every individual and fosters peace and harmony.

4. **Upholding honesty:** The Bible places a high value on honesty and integrity, condemning deception for personal gain. Whether through lies, cheating, or omission, dishonesty is at odds with Christian values and is pervasive in various spheres of life.

5. **Leading a moral life:** Living morally involves recognizing that our bodies are temples of the Holy Spirit and should be honored accordingly. Moral conduct encompasses refraining from evil thoughts, murder, adultery, theft, false testimony, slander, greed, and other vices.

6. **Cultivating generosity:** The Bible exhorts believers to share generously with those in need, emphasizing the reciprocal nature of giving and receiving. Acts of generosity include donating time, money, and resources to charitable causes and needy individuals.

7. **Practicing authenticity:** Authenticity involves aligning one's words and actions, avoiding hypocrisy. The Bible condemns self-righteousness and underscores the importance of practicing what is preached.

8. **Abstaining from retaliation:** Jesus rejected the concept of retaliation and revenge, encouraging a nonresistant attitude toward those who harm us. Hatred and revenge have no place in the life of a Christian.

9. **Forgiving others:** Forgiveness is a central theme in the Bible, reflecting God's mercy toward humanity. Just as God forgives our transgressions, Christians are called to forgive those who wrong them.

10. **Seeking spiritual growth:** The Bible advocates continuous spiritual growth and transformation. As individuals embrace these values, they embark on a journey toward personal and communal flourishing.

All in all, the Bible underscores these values as crucial principles for leading a life that aligns with divine intentions. By adhering to these principles, we can foster compassion, harmony, and fulfillment in our lives and communities.

## *Core Islamic Values*

Summing up Islam's core values is challenging, yet Prophet Muhammad identified pivotal beliefs and practices widely agreed upon by Muslims.

Muslim scholars also discern Quranic teachings, Prophet Muhammad's insights, and Shariah essentials.

*Core Beliefs (Six Articles of Faith)*

1. **Monotheism:** Serve only Allah, shunning the worship of others. The gravest sin is associating partners with Allah.

2. **Angels:** Unseen angels serve Allah, recording our deeds.

3. **Prophets:** Prophets convey God's guidance, culminating in Muhammad, stressing monotheism.

4. **Revealed books:** Scriptures, like the Bible and Torah, offer wisdom; the Quran's finality is preserved.

5. **Day of Judgment:** All face judgment, rewarded or punished based on faith and actions.

6. **Divine Decree:** God's will reigns; our choices, known to Him, coexist with free will (Mufti, 2013).

*Core Practices (Five Pillars of Islam)*

1. **Declaration of faith:** Acknowledge God's oneness and Muhammad's prophethood; embody them in actions.

2. **Daily prayer:** Five formal prayers unite Muslims with God's strength and tranquility.

3. **Zakah (charity):** Wealthy aid the needy, acknowledging wealth as a divine blessing.

4. **Fast of Ramadan:** Annual fasting cultivates self-control, empathy, and devotion.

5. **Hajj pilgrimage:** A sacred journey to Mecca, a profound spiritual experience (Mufti, 2013).

## Other Core Beliefs

- Surah al-Fatihah, the Quran's first chapter, is pivotal and recited in prayers. It praises God's mercy, sovereignty, and guidance on the righteous path.

- Classical scholars condensed Muhammad's teachings, fostering intention-driven actions, purity, compassion, and detachment from materialism.

- Shariah prioritizes religion, life, family, mind, and wealth. It suggests justice or liberty. These essentials ensure human welfare.

In its essence, Islam encapsulates a profound call to wholeheartedly devote oneself to the unwavering service, worship, and tender submission to the divine presence of Allah. This fundamental concept beckons believers to embrace a life of profound devotion, wherein every facet of existence is intertwined with a deep-seated commitment to honor and revere Allah. It signifies a continuous journey of the heart and soul, where acts of worship and submission become not only rituals but a heartfelt expression of love and reverence toward the Creator.

Chapter 4:

# Messengers of Divine Wisdom

Throughout the pages of human history, a remarkable thread emerges—that of the prophets, who serve as messengers of divine wisdom. These extraordinary individuals, handpicked by the Creator, assume the role of intermediaries between the celestial and the Earthly, bearing sacred revelations that cast a guiding light upon humanity's path.

From the Torah to the New Testament Gospels, and from the Quran to the pages of faith, the function of prophets exceeds the boundaries of mortal existence. It molds belief systems, shapes moral conduct, and forges an unbreakable bridge connecting the celestial and human realms.

In this chapter, we examine these spiritual luminaries. We shall delve into their life stories, decipher their profound messages, and unravel the miracles that underscore their celestial communion. All the while, we shall unearth the timeless wisdom they bestow upon the world at large.

## Role and Function of the Prophets

Within the faiths, spanning across Judaism, Christianity, and Islam, a profound unity thrives—a shared conviction that the Creator—God—has engaged in a sacred dialogue with humanity throughout the ages. The term "revelation," a concept derived from the essence of "reveal," unveils truths, making them visible and manifest (*God and prophets*, 2020).

Emanating from this shared conviction is the fundamental belief of all monotheistic traditions: Almighty God, in His boundless wisdom, chose to unveil Himself to select people, known as prophets, through the passage of time.

United by this belief, adherents of Judaism, Christianity, and Islam perceive the dissemination of five central messages through divine revelation (*God and prophets*, 2020):

1. **The essence of the divine:** At the core of these revelations lies an illumination of the nature and attributes of the singular, omnipotent God—the foundation of all existence.

2. **Cosmic design and purpose:** The revelations unravel the intricate web of the universe, unveiling the purpose behind its creation and the Divine intention that guides its course.

3. **Sole deity and worship:** Across these faiths resonates a clarion call to worship the one true God, casting aside all others and embracing unwavering devotion.

4. **Human destiny and ethical living:** Divine communication proclaims the profound purpose of human life—a call to righteous living, the anticipation of posthumous judgment, and the promise of retribution or reward in the afterlife.

5. **Guidance for righteous conduct:** The sacred messages bring forth a luminous code of ethics and laws, a roadmap for us to navigate the complexities of a moral existence.

Amid this rich convergence, prophets emerge as the chosen conduits of these revelations—mortal vessels entrusted with the sacred task of delivering divine wisdom to their fellow humans. Adamantly affirming their roles, these luminaries forge an indelible connection between the earthly and the divine.

Rooted in the heart of Abrahamic faiths lies the resounding truth that prophets, though human, are divinely selected emissaries tasked with conveying revelations to their fellow humans. This sacred transference of wisdom from the divine realm to the Earthly is a cornerstone shared among monotheistic traditions.

Central to this belief is the recognition that certain eminent prophets received monumental revelations—profound insights etched into the collective memory of humanity through recitation, transcription, and preservation within holy scriptures spanning the passage of centuries. Yet, the divine calling of prophets extends beyond the pages of scripture; it ignites the flames of inspiration within their hearts, compelling them to impart profound truths to all of humanity.

Abraham takes center stage in the symphony of prophets, a towering figure casting his shadow across the expanse of all monotheistic creeds. While pivotal, he is not the inaugural recipient of divine revelation. Instead, the honor of this inaugural interaction belongs to the primordial pair—Adam and Eve—the first recipients of celestial discourse.

At the dawn of creation, it was not Abraham but rather Adam and Eve who first received the celestial whisperings—an embodiment of divine communion. Amid the constellation of prophetic luminaries, the names of Elijah, Isaiah, Noah, Jonah, Abraham, Jacob, Moses, David, and Solomon shimmer as constellations, each radiating unique spiritual insights.

Yet, as unity harmonizes with diversity, so too does variation emerge. Distinct interpretations of the prophetic realm arise surrounding two particular figures—Jesus and Muhammad. These two eminent figures evoke divergent narratives, spanning a temporal expanse of about 600 years.

Among these luminous threads, only within the embrace of Islam is Muhammad hailed as the final prophet. Born in Mecca circa 570, he is revered as the vessel through which God's ultimate revelation—a beacon of divine wisdom—was delivered to humanity, crystallized within the sacred pages of the Quran (*God and prophets,* 2020).

In this symphony of revelation and prophecy, these Abrahamic faiths weave a harmonious yet diverse narrative, wherein prophets stand as conduits of heavenly discourse and harbingers of divine wisdom—a timeless testament to the bridge that spans the Earthly and the celestial, and the human and the divine.

## Key Prophets in Judaism

- **Moses:** An iconic and pivotal figure in Judaism, Moses stands as the central leader who guided the Israelites from the depths of Egyptian slavery to the threshold of the Promised Land. His profound connection with the Divine was exemplified on Mount Sinai, where he received the Torah, a sacred covenant that established the bedrock of Jewish identity and principles. Moses' journey epitomizes courage, resilience, and unwavering commitment to fulfilling God's purpose.

- **Abraham:** Revered as the patriarch and foundational ancestor of Judaism, Abraham's legacy is etched in his unyielding faith and profound covenant with the Almighty. His remarkable willingness to sacrifice his beloved son, Isaac, in obedience to God's command underscores his unwavering devotion. Abraham's spiritual lineage reverberates through generations, embodying a testament to the enduring relationship between humanity and the divine. His life narrative continues to inspire seekers of truth and exemplifies the profound impact of a life that aligns with God's will.

- **Isaiah:** The prophetic voice of Isaiah resounds through the ages, echoing messages of hope, social justice, and the promise of a brighter future. His visionary pronouncements, chronicled in The Book of Isaiah, unveil a glimpse of a world characterized by righteousness and harmony. Isaiah's profound influence shapes Jewish thought and theology, emphasizing the intersection of divine providence and human responsibility. His teachings provide a guiding light for navigating the complexities of faith and righteous living.

- **Jeremiah:** Jeremiah emerges as a resolute and compassionate prophet who confronted his people with calls for introspection and inner renewal. His poignant exhortations, often delivered against a backdrop of impending calamity, emphasize the profound impact of personal transformation. Jeremiah's prophetic mission embodies a relentless pursuit of spiritual revival and a heartfelt plea to return to God's path. His legacy underscores the transformative power of aligning one's heart with divine principles.

- **Elijah:** The indomitable spirit of Elijah symbolizes fervent devotion to the divine and the embodiment of divine intervention. His role as a miracle worker and unwavering defender of monotheism solidified his status as a revered prophet. In Jewish eschatology, the anticipation of Elijah's return heralds the dawn of a messianic era marked by ultimate redemption and restoration. Elijah's narrative encapsulates unshakable faith, steadfast resolve, and a profound commitment to fulfilling God's purposes (*Ancient Jewish history,* n.d.).

In the rich mosaic of Jewish prophetic heritage, these central figures shine as beacons of faith, exemplifying courage, dedication, and the profound impact of a life lived in communion with God's guidance. Their stories continue to inspire and guide us on our spiritual journey, offering timeless wisdom and lessons for future generations.

## Key Prophets in Christianity

- **Jesus Christ:** The focal point of Christianity revolves around Jesus Christ, a prominent figure revered as the embodiment of Divine revelation. He holds diverse roles as a prophet, Messiah, and the cherished Son of God. Through his profound teachings, Jesus illuminated the pathway of love, forgiveness, and salvation, inviting believers into a transformative connection with the Divine. His sacrificial demise and triumphant resurrection stand as the pivotal axis upon which the Christian faith hinges, ushering in a fresh era of grace and eternal optimism.

- **John the Baptist:** John the Baptist emerges as a precursor, heralding the imminent arrival of Jesus' life-altering ministry. His prophetic voice resonated with a call to repentance, symbolized through baptism, preparing hearts for the profound message of Christ. John's role as a forerunner to Jesus underscores his vital part in preparing the way for a spiritual reawakening and the initiation of a new covenant anchored in redemption.

- **Jeremiah:** Within Christianity, Jeremiah's prophetic heritage finds resonance in his profound insights into the dawn of a new covenant and the heralding of Jesus' advent. His prophetic declarations foretell a future marked by divine transformation and the pledge of reconciliation through the Messiah. Jeremiah's enduring influence extends to Christian theology, enriching understandings of God's redeeming plan and fulfilling ancient prophecies.

- **Daniel:** The visionary revelations of Daniel unveil a panorama of prophetic revelations that cast light on the grand idea of God's unfolding design. His foresight into the arrival of the Son of Man and the establishment of an eternal kingdom resonates profoundly within Christian belief. Daniel's prophecies invite adherents to contemplate the Divine narrative of history, brimming with assurances of divine intervention and the triumph of God's sovereign rule.

- **Peter and the Apostles:** The apostles, notably Peter, emerge as steadfast pillars in Christianity's early underpinnings, instrumental in disseminating Jesus' teachings and advancing the Gospel's transformative message. Their unwavering commitment to spreading the Good News is a testament to Divine revelation's enduring impact. Christian communities were nurtured through their endeavors, and the foundations of faith were established, showcasing the potency of prophetic inspiration in shaping and rallying nascent believers (*Prophets of God*, 2011).

In the Christian tradition, these pivotal prophets and figures interlace to form a dynamic tableau of faith, inspiration, and

Divine guidance. Their contributions have indelibly molded the contours of Christian theology and spirituality, inviting adherents to traverse the path of redemption, compassion, and steadfast devotion.

## Key Prophets in Islam

- **Moses:** Referred to as Musa in Islam, holds a significant role within the faith, leading the Israelites away from the bonds of Egyptian slavery, receiving Divine revelation in the form of the Torah, and guiding his people on the journey to the Promised Land. His unwavering commitment to God's guidance and his role as a prophet of Islam underscores his profound influence on the faith. Moses' life is characterized by his pivotal interactions with the Pharaoh of Egypt, his reception of the Ten Commandments, and his tireless efforts to guide the Israelites toward righteous living.

- **Noah:** Renowned in Islamic tradition as 'Nuh,' Noah's narrative resonates as a testament to patience, faith, and unwavering devotion to Allah's commands. His prophetic mission was marked by the divine directive to construct an ark to safeguard righteous believers and animals from an impending flood—a monumental trial that underscored his steadfastness. Despite widespread disbelief and ridicule from his people, Noah's adherence to his prophetic duty showcases his embodiment of resilience and his ultimate reliance on Allah's wisdom.

- **Abraham:** Revered as 'Ibrahim' in Islam, Abraham emerges as a patriarchal figure whose unwavering monotheistic devotion earned him the title of 'Friend of

God.' His refusal to bow to idols and his resolute pursuit of the true God distinguish him as a beacon of faith. Muslims regard Abraham as the father of two esteemed prophets, Isaac and Ishmael, embodying familial lineage that carries the message of monotheism and submission to Allah's will.

- **Jesus:** Affectionately known as 'Isa' in Islam, Jesus occupies a revered place as a virtuous messenger of Allah, characterized by his miraculous birth, prophetic ministry, and divine miracles. Islam upholds Jesus as a faithful messenger who healed the infirm, restored sight to the blind, and even raised the dead through Allah's Divine intervention. While Muslims diverge from the Christian belief in Jesus' divinity and crucifixion, his teachings of compassion, humility, and love remain cherished aspects of his prophetic legacy.

- **Muhammad:** The cornerstone of Islam, Prophet Muhammad's life is a beacon of guidance for Muslims worldwide. His birth in 570 marked the beginning of an extraordinary prophetic journey that culminated in the revelation of the Quran. Embodying the virtues of trustworthiness and integrity from a young age, Muhammad earned the title of "Al-Amin"—the trustworthy one. When he was 40 years old, the pivotal moment of divine revelation through the Archangel Gabriel set the stage for a transformative 23-year period during which the Quran unfolded, serving as a comprehensive guide for life. Muhammad's enduring impact is marked by his efforts to unify the diverse Arabian tribes under the banner of monotheism, paving the way for the birth of Islam as a comprehensive way of life (Huda, 2018).

In the vibrant Islamic faith and belief, these key prophets are intertwined with unwavering commitment, Divine guidance, and a shared mission to illuminate the path of submission and devotion to Allah.

Their profound stories, teachings, and legacies continue to shape the spiritual landscape of Islam, inspiring adherents to uphold the values of monotheism, compassion, and righteous living.

## Signs and Miracles

Within the sacred pages of the Torah, a plethora of breathtaking miracles unfolds, weaving a narrative that reverberates with divine potency. Among them, the astonishing parting of the Red Sea emerges as an undeniable testament to the authority of the Divine.

The plagues that descended upon Egypt, defying natural laws, serve as a vivid reminder of Moses' extraordinary conduit to the supernatural. Adding to this tapestry, the miraculous provision of manna in the desert showcases otherworldly sustenance that nourished the Israelites on their arduous journey, deepening the connection between Moses and the Creator (*Three natural miracles,* 2013).

The Gospels unfurl a tableau of miracles attributed to Jesus, spotlighting his commanding sovereignty and boundless compassion. These wonders, spanning from the restoration of the afflicted to the transformation of water into wine, encapsulate the profound depth of Jesus' Divine authority. At its zenith, the resurrection of Jesus stands as an unassailable testament to his conquest over mortality, laying the unshakable foundation of faith.

The pages of the Quran unveil a gallery of miracles that resonate with celestial grandeur, solidifying their status as unmistakable tokens of God's presence. Among them, the awe-inspiring splitting of the moon bears witness to Allah's sovereignty over the celestial sphere.

The sudden gushing forth of water from an arid rock exemplifies divine providence flourishing even in the most parched of landscapes. Anchoring this narrative, preserving Prophet Muhammad's fingerprint on a stone becomes a tangible relic of the sacred, bridging the earthly with the celestial in an intricate tapestry.

Miracles emerge as irrefutable markers of celestial intervention, offering tangible evidence of prophetic legitimacy. Beyond their stunning displays, these miracles substantiate the authenticity of divine messages, nurturing unswerving faith in believers' hearts. The gravity of these extraordinary occurrences leaves an enduring imprint, reinforcing the conviction that transcends the ordinary and delves into the extraordinary realm.

While miracles are indeed extraordinary, their significance extends beyond the surface, carrying profound spiritual truths. Each miraculous event serves as a guiding light, illuminating facets of the divine character—a living embodiment of omnipotence, compassion, and boundless mercy.

Whether parting waters or coaxing life from the barren rock, miracles resonate as symbolic revelations, beckoning contemplation into the profound mysteries of the divine. Miracles stand as tangible manifestations of the ineffable, affirming the presence of the miraculous within the confines of human existence.

Across the Torah, Bible, and Quran, the resonance of miracles resounds as a resounding affirmation of divine engagement with humanity. Far from mundane, these remarkable occurrences leave an indelible mark on the canvas of faith, serving as unwavering testimony to the juncture of humans and the celestial.

# Chapter 5:

# Connecting With the Divine Through Prayer and Ritual

Religion imparts the wisdom that prayer might not always yield immediate results, suggesting that God's responses aren't guaranteed with every petition. However, it's important to remember that God does indeed engage with every prayer we sincerely offer from the depths of our hearts.

Authenticity is key; we cannot conceal anything from God, as He already comprehends our innermost struggles and joys. One of the most impactful techniques to commune with Him involves immersing ourselves in His teachings. Through dedicated reading and contemplation of the Scriptures, we unlock the channel to directly receive His guidance and answers.

## Forms and Times of Prayer

The assurance of His presence is affirmed when His words align with the sacred text and grant us a profound sense of serenity. To truly hear God, we must diligently filter out internal and external distractions, enabling our undivided focus on Him.

This requires both external quietude and inner tranquility. In the realm of Abrahamic faiths, there are both shared elements and unique practices in how adherents pray and connect with the Creator.

## Jewish Prayers

Engraved within the fabric of Jewish law is the sacred obligation to pray three times daily: at dawn, during the afternoon, and as twilight descends. These devotions are known as morning prayer (*shacharit*), afternoon prayer (*minchah*), and evening prayer (*arvith* or *maariv*) (Mindel, n.d.).

The ancient wisdom imparted by our venerable sages reveals the origins of the thrice-daily prayer practice, which can be attributed to our esteemed Patriarchs: Abraham, Isaac, and Jacob. This tradition was not merely handed down through generations but was carefully crafted by these patriarchal figures, each leaving their unique mark on the ritual. Abraham, for instance, initiated the morning prayer, infusing it with a distinct significance. Following in his footsteps, Isaac elevated the afternoon prayer to a position of prominence within the tradition. Finally, Jacob enriched the evening devotion with his own distinctive contributions, thus completing the triad of daily spiritual connection. This historical account underscores the deliberate and purposeful evolution of our prayer tradition over time (Mindel, n.d.).

The Zohar, a profound work that intricately explores the core of Torah and Chabad philosophy, provides a deeper understanding of this concept. Within their teachings, a fascinating revelation emerges: Each of the Patriarchs is a unique symbol of a fundamental quality that profoundly influenced their devotion to the Divine. Abraham stands as the embodiment of love, Isaac personifies awe, and Jacob radiates mercy. These insights shed light on the spiritual dimensions of their respective journeys, enriching our comprehension of their divine service (Mindel, n.d.).

Though not exclusive to anyone, each figure had more pronounced qualities. Abraham's kindness and love, Isaac's strict justice and reverence, and Jacob's harmonious blend of the two paved the way for their descendants to connect with God through love, awe, and compassion. Mercy becomes poignant when we acknowledge the soul's connection to the Creator and feel compassion for its frequent distractions amidst the material aspects of daily life.

At Mount Sinai, as the Torah was bestowed upon us by God, our way of life was meticulously outlined. The Torah, meaning "teaching," "instruction," and "guidance," encompasses 613 commandments. The mandate stands among them to "serve God with all our heart and soul" (Mindel, n.d.).

To fulfill this command, we turn to prayer, not only obeying the commandment to pray but also kindling the flames of love and awe for God, separate yet intertwined directives.

In the first millennia since the era of Moses, prayer did not adhere to a fixed structure. While the imperative of daily prayer was established, the specifics of form and frequency were left to individual discretion. However, a structured order of service emerged in the sacred precincts of the Holy Temple in Jerusalem, the Beit Hamikdash.

Daily sacrifices punctuated the morning and evening hours, stretching into the night. Special occasions, such as Shabbos and festivals, witnessed supplementary offerings, potentially inspiring personal thrice-daily prayers.

Prominently, King David avowed his devotion through thrice-daily prayer, and even Daniel, in far-off Babylon, turned toward Jerusalem for his prayers thrice daily. The remnants of public worship, symbolized by Beit Ha'am, were present in the era of the first Temple, though ravaged by the Babylonian destruction of Jerusalem and its sacred edifice.

Following the destruction of the Holy Temple and the subsequent exile to Babylon, the flame of communal prayer persisted. In foreign lands, the congregational prayers transformed gathering places into sanctuaries, Beit Mikdash Me'at. Amidst linguistic diversity, the descendants of Babylonian exiles grappled with a fractured Hebrew tongue.

Upon their return from exile, guided by Ezra the Scribe and a council of prophets and sages known as the Great Assembly, the text of the daily prayer, Shemoneh Esrei, the "Eighteen Benedictions," was standardized. This eternal script etched its place in Jewish life, echoing the rhythm of daily Temple sacrifices (Mindel, n.d.).

Imprinted with the wisdom of our sages, these prayers endure as a timeless legacy. Verses like Shema and Shemoneh Esrei, eternal gems, grace morning and evening devotionals.

Amidst this symphony, the resonance of the Holy Temple resounds, and the Psalms of David, once sung by Levites within its sacred walls, enrich the morning prayer. Within this unbroken continuum, our prayers unfold as a testament to the enduring spirit of faith, echoing through the corridors of history.

## *Christian Prayers*

Prayer is an essential part of Christianity, yet we often grapple with integrating it consistently into our daily lives. Part of the challenge lies in the misconception that prayer has only one prescribed form.

What are the various prayer types depicted in the Bible? While there are numerous forms of prayer, seven major categories emerge, each accompanied by relevant scriptures.

These are the primary prayer types (ORBC, 2021):

1. **Prayer of worship:** At its core, worshipful prayer centers on acknowledging God's greatness. It entails recognizing His immense power and majesty. This can range from simple expressions like "God, you are magnificent" to profound declarations, as found in Revelation 4:11: "You are worthy, our Lord and God, to receive glory and honor and power, for you created all things, and by your will they existed and were created" (*New International Version*, 2011/1973, Revelation 4:11).

2. **Prayer of thanksgiving:** Expressing gratitude to the Father for the blessings in our lives constitutes a form of prayer closely related to worship. While worship emphasizes God's nature, thanksgiving centers on appreciating His deeds. Psalms 100:4 succinctly encapsulates both aspects: "Enter his gates with thanksgiving, and his courts with praise! Give thanks to him; bless his name" (*New International Version*, 2011/1973, Psalms 100:4).

3. **Prayer of faith:** This prayer reflects our unwavering trust in God's will. Rather than imposing our desires, we submit to His plan. James 5:13–16 offers insight: "Is anyone among you in trouble? Let them pray… The prayer offered in faith will make the sick person well" (*New International Version*, 2011/1973, James 5:13–16).

4. **Prayer of intercession:** When we intercede, we pray on behalf of others. A notable instance is seen in Daniel 9:1–27, where Daniel implores for his people's well-

being (*New International Version*, 2011/1973, Daniel 9:1–27). This practice emphasizes caring for the needs of others through prayer.

5. **Corporate prayer:** Engaging in prayer as a group fosters unity and community among believers. Acts 12:5–18 illustrates corporate prayer within the church context, as they fervently pray for Peter's safety (*New International Version*, 2011/1973, Acts 12:5–18).

6. **Prayer of consecration:** Communion embodies this prayer form. During communion, we consecrate the elements, requesting God's sanctification. Matthew 26:26–27 portrays Jesus consecrating the bread and wine, signifying their sacredness (*New International Version*, 2011/1973, Matthew 26:26–27).

7. **Prayer of the Holy Spirit:** When we lack clarity in our prayers, the Holy Spirit aids us. Romans 8:26–27 affirms the Spirit's role in interceding for us according to God's will (*New International Version*, 2011/1973, Romans 8:26–27).

Dispelling the notion of a "right way" to pray, the key is authenticity. Honesty in dialogue with God is the essence of proper prayer. God welcomes our genuine emotions—anger, grief, and fear. He accompanies us on our journey, nurturing our growth.

To nurture our relationship with God, constant prayer is vital. Although achieving this may take time, striving for ongoing communication strengthens our spiritual bond.

## *Muslim Prayers*

For Muslims, the five daily prayer sessions, known as salat, hold significant importance within the Islamic faith. These prayers serve as a means to connect with God, seek His guidance, and seek forgiveness. Additionally, they reinforce the sense of shared faith and rituals among Muslims globally. Let's delve into the process of Muslim prayer and its rituals.

Initiating their prayers, Islam teaches its followers to embrace a profound connection between their mental focus and physical purification. The pivotal preparatory step involves a ritual known as "wudhu," which mandates the thorough cleansing of hands, feet, arms, and legs before the act of prayer can take place (Huda, 2019). Additionally, adhering to a dress code of modest attire is imperative, signifying the significance of approaching prayer with both inner devotion and outward reverence.

Once *wudhu* is completed, worshippers find a suitable location for prayer. Although many opt for mosques to engage in communal prayer, any tranquil space, whether within a home or office, suffices. The critical requirement is to face Mecca, the birthplace of Prophet Muhammad, during prayer (Huda, 2019).

### *The Ritual of Prayer*

Typically performed on a small prayer rug, although not obligatory, prayers involve reciting prescribed phrases in Arabic alongside a sequence of ritualistic postures. These postures, known as *Rak'ah*, are designed to glorify Allah and express devotion. The number of *Rak'ahs* varies from two to four, depending on the time of day (Huda, 2019):

- **Takbir:** Standing with hands raised to shoulder level, worshippers declare "Allahu Akbar" (God is great).

- **Qiyaam:** While still standing, the faithful cross their right arm over the left on their chest or navel. Reciting the Quran's first chapter, along with other supplications, follows.

- **Ruku:** Bowing toward Mecca, hands rest on knees as the phrase "Glory be to God, the greatest" is repeated three times.

- **Second Qiyaam:** Returning to a standing position with arms at sides, Allah's glory is proclaimed again.

- **Sujud:** Kneeling with only specific body parts touching the ground, worshippers declare "Glory be to God, the highest" thrice.

- **Tashahhud:** Transitioning to a seated posture, feet beneath them and hands on laps, provides a moment for reflection.

- **Second Sujud:** Kneeling is repeated.

- **Second Tashahhud:** Further prayers to Allah are offered, and devotion is affirmed by briefly raising the right index finger. Forgiveness and mercy are also sought.

If congregational, prayers conclude with mutual messages of peace. Worshippers turn to their right and left, exchanging the greeting, "Peace be upon you, and the mercy and blessings of Allah."

## Prayer Timings

In Muslim communities, daily calls to prayer (*adhan*) remind people of salat times. A designated caller of prayer (*muezzin*) recites the Takbir and the Kalimah from the mosque's minaret. These calls were once unamplified but are now often amplified for clarity. The sun's position determines prayer timings (Huda, 2019):

- **Fajr:** Before sunrise, this prayer marks the start of the day.

- **Dhuhr:** Shortly after midday, this prayer offers a pause for reflection.

- **'Asr:** In the late afternoon, a moment of contemplation arrives.

- **Maghrib:** As the sun sets, this prayer signifies the close of the day.

- **'Isha:** Before retiring for the night, this final prayer invokes God's presence, guidance, mercy, and forgiveness.

While devout Muslims consider missing prayers a significant lapse, circumstances may arise. Tradition suggests making up missed prayers promptly or including them in the subsequent regular salat.

## Rituals of Purification

Ritual purification is a religious practice intended to remove a state of uncleanliness before engaging in worship or sacred activities. This concept is prevalent in various religions and involves specific rituals to achieve a state of ritual purity.

Ritual impurity is distinct from ordinary physical dirt and can apply to individuals, objects, and places. In some religions, certain body fluids are considered ritually unclean. Let's explore how ritual purification is observed in different faiths:

- **Biblical rituals of purification:** In the Bible, various purification rituals are outlined, including those related to menstruation, childbirth, sexual relations, bodily emissions, skin diseases, death, and animal sacrifices. For instance, the Ethiopian Orthodox Tewahedo Church has specific hand-washing practices after using the latrine, before prayer, and after meals. In this tradition, women are restricted from entering the church during menstruation, and men refrain from entering a church after sexual relations.

- **Baptism in Christianity:** Baptism serves as a form of ritual purification in Christianity. It is practiced in several branches of Christianity, symbolizing spiritual cleansing and rebirth. Baptism entails being immersed or sprinkled with water and is significant in the forgiveness of sins.

- **Islamic ritual purification:** In Islam, ritual purification is integral to preparing for salah, the ritual prayer. It involves practices like ablution (*wudu*) and full-body washing (*ghusl*) using water. The form of purification varies based on circumstances, such as menstruation, post-sexual activity, or the absence of water. Certain acts, like flatulence and unconsciousness, can break the state of ritual purity.

- **Jewish laws of purity:** In Judaism, ritual purity is observed through practices like hand washing as well as immersion in a mikvah ritual bath. The laws of purity encompass various situations, including menstruation, childbirth, sexual relations, and contact with corpses.

Purification is essential for engaging in holy activities and entering sacred spaces.

- **Ritual impurity of death:** *Tumat HaMet* in Judaism pertains to contact with a human corpse, signifying the highest degree of impurity. It requires a unique purification process involving the ashes of the red heifer. Although the practical implications are limited today, the concept still holds significance in Jewish tradition.

- **Reformed Christianity:** In Reformed Christianity, ritual purity is achieved through confession of sins, assurance of forgiveness, and sanctification. The emphasis is on offering one's being as a "living sacrifice" and maintaining a clean way of life.

- **Observance and variations:** The observance and details of ritual purification can vary among different denominations and schools of thought within each religion. While some traditions adhere strictly to purification rituals, others may adapt or reinterpret them over time (*Ritual purification*, n.d.).

Ritual purification serves to spiritually prepare and cleanse oneself before engaging in religious activities. It reflects the importance of inner and outer cleanliness, reverence, and devotion in various faith traditions.

## Sacred Spaces and Places

This section explores the holy spaces of worship and places of pilgrimage for the three Abrahamic religions.

## *Jewish Worship and Sacred Sites*

Israel holds profound, multifaceted importance for Jews, intricately tied to their history, spirituality, and culture. Jerusalem, a city of great significance, houses sacred sites central to Jewish identity.

The Western Wall, or Kotel, is a potent symbol of Jewish faith and resilience. This ancient remnant of the Second Temple links past and present, drawing pilgrims to connect, pray, and find solace. It embodies Jewish heritage, with ties to the Ark of the Covenant and the Ten Commandments.

Synagogues are pivotal in daily Jewish life. Beyond worship, they foster community, education, and growth. Synagogues vary in design but share key elements (*Uri kids,* n.d.):

- **Holy Ark:** Houses Torah scrolls, connecting to Jewish scripture
- **Star of David:** Symbolizing faith and identity
- **Eternal light:** Represents God's enduring presence and worship
- **Reading table:** Facilitates Torah study and communal reflection
- **Ten Commandments replica:** Emphasizes ethical principles
- **Rabbi's seat:** Signifies leadership and guidance

Synagogue services, led by a rabbi and cantor, blend prayer, song, and study. Torah readings and sermons offer spiritual nourishment.

Israel's historical and spiritual significance, the Western Wall's symbolism, and vibrant synagogue life all contribute to the rich tapestry of Jewish faith and tradition.

## Christian Worship and Sacred Sites

Christian worship predominantly occurs in churches, serving as spaces for communal devotion, reflection, and connection with God. Worship occurs primarily on Sundays, with additional gatherings for special occasions and festivals. Ordained priests, pastors, or ministers often lead church services and include participatory elements such as prayers, hymns, readings, and sermons. The Holy Eucharist, symbolizing Christ's sacrifice, holds a central place in many services.

Church architecture varies, but common features include a bell tower, nave (seating area), altar, pulpit, lectern, choir loft, stained glass windows, candles, and baptismal font.

### *Christian Holy Sites*

- **Jerusalem:** A city of profound religious importance for Christians, Jews, and Muslims. Key Christian sites include the Hill of Golgotha (crucifixion site), the Church of the Holy Sepulcher (burial and resurrection), the Garden of Gethsemane (prayer and betrayal), and the Hall of the Last Supper.

- **Bethlehem:** Birthplace of Jesus, home to the Church of the Nativity (birth site) and the Milk Grotto (refuge of the Holy Family).

- **Sephoria:** Potential hometown of Mary's parents, featuring an ancient synagogue and Christian ruins.

- **Sea of Galilee:** Significant for Jesus' miracles and teachings. Includes Capernaum (Jesus' residence), the Garden of Tabgha (miraculous feeding), and the Mount of Beatitudes (Sermon on the Mount).

- **Nazareth:** Jesus' hometown, with sites like the Basilica of the Annunciation (angel's announcement), Synagogue Church (early teachings), and St. Joseph's Church (Joseph's workshop) (*URI kids,* n.d.).

These sacred sites draw Christian pilgrims seeking spiritual connection, renewal, and a deeper understanding of their faith by engaging with the life and teachings of Jesus Christ.

## Islamic Worship and Sacred Sites

Muslim worship centers around mosques, which are vital to spiritual and communal life. While daily prayers occur in various places, mosques are central for congregational and Friday prayers.

### *Mosque Architecture*

- **Sahn (courtyard):** Open area for ablutions before prayer

- **Minaret:** Tower for the call to prayer

- **Mihrab:** Niche indicating Mecca's direction

- **Minbar:** Pulpit for sermons

- **Prayer hall (zulla):** Main gathering space

Islamic art decorates mosques with geometric patterns and calligraphy, reflecting the avoidance of images. Stars and crescents symbolize Islam's lunar calendar and divine signs (*Sacred space*, n.d.).

## *Significant Islamic Holy Sites*

- **Prophet's Mosque (Medina):** Resting place of Prophet Muhammad, a site of intercession on the Day of Judgment.

- **Al-Aqsa Mosque (Jerusalem):** Linked to the Night Journey and Ascension of the Prophet, one of Islam's holiest sites.

- **Dome of the Rock (Jerusalem):** Symbolic site of the Prophet's ascent into heaven, though not a mosque.

- **Grand Mosque and Kaaba (Mecca):** Kaaba, built by Adam and rebuilt by Abraham and Ishmael, is central to Muslim unity and worship.

- **Shrines of Sufi and Shi'i Saints:** Shrines over tombs of holy individuals hold spiritual power and blessings.

These sacred spaces anchor Islamic worship, guiding prayers, rituals, and pilgrimages. Their stories and teachings profoundly impact the faith and devotion of Muslims worldwide (*Sacred space*, n.d.).

# Role of Chanting and Recitation

Our bodies consist of vibrating energies; disrupted cell movement leads to disease. Chanting restores cell harmony, resonates with chakras, and brings balance, joy, and peace.

Islamic belief sees chanting as a connection with Allah; faith enhances mantra power.

*Vird*, Urdu chanting, strengthens ties with Allah. During namaz or meditation, *vird* demands understanding, love, and concentration.

Islamic chants, like *Duas*, address challenges and healing. Examples: Allahu Akbar, Ya Salaam, Bismillah Al-Rahman, Al-Rahim, Ya Ali Madad, and Allaahumma Innee As a Luka BI-Ismika (Bahri, 2023).

## *Benefits of Chanting*

- **Ego dissolution:** Mantras release self, spreading positivity.

- **Improved brain function:** Regular chanting enhances memory and concentration.

- **Calmness:** Chanting induces calmness and silence.

- **Energy boost:** Chanting energizes and accelerates healing.

- **Divine connection:** Mantras invoke blessings, connecting with the divine.

- **Chanting God's name as a mantra:** Different traditions hold names of God, representing aspects of ultimate reality. Belief amplifies mantra power (Bahri, 2023).

## Christian Chants: Tranquility and Divine Connection

Sacred chants hold a pivotal role in Christian worship. Chants soothe, calm emotions, and connect with the divine.

- **Chanting styles:** Gregorian chant is prominent, evolving over centuries.
- **Features:** Monodic, sung without instruments, and unify worshipers.
- **Chanting the divine name:** "Jesus Prayer," like the Divine Name practice, fosters constant God-awareness (Prabhu, 2008).

## Chanting the Path to Unity: The Power of Jewish Chants

- Shema Yisrael prayer unveils unity; Hebrew chanting enhances understanding.
- Hebrew chants transform words into healing vessels through intention, repetition, and awareness.

- Chanting differs from song, using intention, repetition, and awareness.

Steps (Gold, 2022)

1. Select the sacred phrase.
2. Create a melody.
3. Repeat with intention.
4. Enter silence, breathe, and embrace transformation.

Chanting bridges ancestral wisdom with modern seekers, uniting sacred words with life's journey.

# Chapter 6:

# Spiritual Journey Seeking God's Presence

While a spiritual awakening is often metaphorically described as a journey, it does not entail physical travel or pilgrimage. Instead, it signifies a process of surpassing one's existing boundaries and progressing toward the next level of evolution.

In the course of a human lifespan, only a few encounters hold the potential for a profound and transformative impact as that of a spiritual awakening. The act of recognizing and directly encountering one's inherent divinity marks a monumental shift in perspective.

A spiritual awakening possesses the power to dismantle the very fabric of reality as it has been understood, propelling an individual into a new existence characterized by conscious expansion and advancement. As the term suggests, one emerges from the slumber of ordinary, mundane, ego-driven awareness into a heightened realm of spiritual consciousness.

Comparable to awakening from a deep slumber, we gain clarity to perceive the former reality as a mere illusion, rendering any regression to the previous state inconceivable.

# Inner Transformation

Religion teaches us that prayer isn't always a guaranteed two-way communication with God, yet God does indeed respond to every heartfelt prayer. Authenticity is paramount, as God sees through pretenses, knowing every aspect of our being. A profound way to connect with God is to meditate on His word.

Through dedicated study of scripture, we can hear His voice guiding us with specific answers in harmony with His teachings and granting us peace. The transformation process requires us to filter out internal and external distractions, focusing on God's guidance and wisdom. This transformational journey is reflected in the practices of various Abrahamic faiths, each uniquely shaping how their members pray and connect with the Creator.

Spiritual transformation carries a dual nature of natural growth and supernatural intervention. Just as humans naturally grow from infancy to adulthood, the Christ life within us flourishes if nurtured. Yet, this transformation is ultimately a work of the Holy Spirit, who guides us into truth and communicates God's depth. While we can open ourselves to this process, its initiation and outcome are beyond our control, much like the wind's unpredictable course.

Saint Paul employs metaphors to illustrate this paradox. He likens Christ's formation in us to the process of an embryo developing in its mother's womb—a mysterious, divinely orchestrated occurrence. Similarly, the concept of metamorphosis, as referenced in Romans 12:2, involves a caterpillar's transformation into a butterfly, a change that transcends cognitive understanding (*New International Version*, 2011/1973, Romans 12:2). These metaphors underscore the mysterious, divine nature of spiritual transformation (Barton, 2022).

Though spiritual transformation is a supernatural process, we play a role in creating conditions for it. Spiritual practices, or disciplines, are not about earning favor or proving superiority but about aligning ourselves with God's work. St. Paul encourages offering our bodies as living sacrifices, surrendering ourselves through these disciplines. These practices prepare us for God's transformative work, cultivating habits of love, peace, and joy in the Holy Spirit.

This transformative journey is best undertaken in the community. As members of the body of Christ, we are interconnected for mutual edification, drawing strength from one another. Paul's teachings on transformation consistently emphasize the importance of community (Barton, 2022). While personal disciplines like solitude and meditation are essential, communal practices like corporate prayer, worship, and serving others are equally vital.

The goal of spiritual transformation isn't merely personal growth; it extends to serving others. Mature spirituality involves obeying Christ's commandments, increasing our capacity to love God and fellow humans. This love-driven transformation propels us to share our faith, exhibit generosity, pursue reconciliation and justice, and contribute positively to society.

Ultimately, Christian spiritual formation aims to glorify God, enrich our lives, and serve others. This purpose-driven journey compels us to labor and struggle with the energy inspired by God's presence within us.

# Judaism: Spiritual Disciplines

In Jewish thought, the concept of holiness, or Kedushah, is intricately linked with the notion of restriction and limitation. This theme is woven throughout various aspects of Jewish tradition, underscoring the sacred nature of specific spaces, times, and practices (*Spiritual discipline in Judaism,* n.d.).

Let's contemplate the synagogue as a space imbued with sanctity. Within the realm of Jewish law, known as "halakhah," a set of regulations extends its influence not only during formal services but also outside those moments. These restrictions serve a profound purpose—they serve to maintain the sanctified ambiance of the sanctuary and act as guardians against any profane or ordinary activities that might erode the inherent holiness of this sacred space (*Spiritual discipline in Judaism,* n.d.).

According to experts, this notion is shown by the "Holy of Holies, the inner sanctum of the sacred Temple that once stood in Jerusalem" (*Spiritual discipline in Judaism,* n.d.). Regarded as the "holiest place" in the world, it paradoxically also has the most restrictions. Followers of Judaism say, "Only one person, the High Priest, on one day of the year, Yom Kippur (the Day of Atonement), was ever allowed to enter this sanctified space" (*Spiritual discipline in Judaism,* n.d.).

Restrictions on creative work similarly mark the observance of Shabbat and Holy Days, a central aspect of their observance in traditional Judaism. These limitations underscore the sanctity of these times and contribute to the spiritual significance of these occasions.

Even within the realm of creation, a divine act of self-limitation known as *tsimtsum* is recognized in Jewish mystical teachings.

This withdrawal of the divine allows room for the existence of the created universe. Although not explicitly termed "holy," *tsimtsum* is regarded as an expression of divine love, essential for the emergence of the world and all that inhabits it (*Spiritual discipline in Judaism*, n.d.).

A common thread in various facets of Jewish faith and practice is the presence of limitation, which forms the foundation of discipline. Love and sexuality, for instance, are consecrated and bound by the marital union's commitment, known as Kiddushin. This commitment imposes restrictions on intimate relations outside marriage, aligning with Jewish law.

Even within a marriage, sexual intimacy is subject to limitations, observed on specific days of the month. A woman's menstrual period and subsequent days impose a temporary restriction, culminating in a ritual immersion known as mikvah. This immersion, often in natural water sources, symbolizes renewal and rebirth, fostering deeper connection and communication between spouses.

Prayer, another integral aspect of Jewish practice, exemplifies the discipline required for spiritual connection. While personal communication with God is possible at any time, formal prayers are meticulously structured by Jewish law and custom. Specific prayers are designated for particular days and times, reflecting a harmonious blend of personal devotion and structured discipline.

Charitable giving, or *tzedakah*, also adheres to the principle of limitation. Jewish teaching advocates donating a portion of income, typically 10%, to assist the needy. This practice of responsible giving underscores the importance of balancing acts of kindness with prudent self-care within the context of spiritual life.

While the desire for spirituality and connection with the divine is unquestionably valuable, these elements are channeled and framed by the framework of religious discipline and halacha restrictions in Judaism. This disciplined approach aims to cultivate an enduring, genuine, and inclusive relationship with the divine, transforming spiritual experiences into a continuous reality accessible to a broad spectrum of believers.

## Islamic Disciplines

As stated in the Quran (*The Holy Quran*, 2016):

> O' you who have true faith! Do not give preference [to your own words and deeds] above those of Allah and His Messenger [the Prophet Muhammad, blessings of Allah be upon him and his progeny]. And have consciousness of Allah. Unquestionably, Allah is the All-Hearing, All-Knowing. (49:1)

This verse aims to establish a sense of moral discipline within every true believer, guiding them to place the commands of Allah and His Messenger above their own desires. This discipline prevents believers from doubting or wavering in their commitment to these divine instructions (Subhani, n.d.).

The principles of Islam dictate that individuals should derive their laws and regulations from the Almighty source, wholeheartedly embracing them above all other ideologies. This is because only the Creator possesses complete knowledge of human nature and is free from error or self-interest. True faith requires trusting Allah's wisdom and adhering to the Islamic disciplines without putting personal wishes before divine guidance.

Failure to uphold this discipline would lead to confusion and disorder in life, much like an army with multiple conflicting leaders. Similarly, societal harmony and justice would deteriorate if individuals prioritized their opinions over divine commands. The verse emphasizes not favoring personal opinions over Allah's guidance, setting the tone for believers to prioritize divine directives over their own desires.

History provides examples of those who favored their own judgments over Allah's commands. During the Prophet's time, some companions hesitated to follow his instructions, showcasing personal preferences over obedience. Similarly, certain early Muslims challenged the Prophet's marriage to Zainab due to cultural biases. These instances highlight the dangers of prioritizing personal opinions over divine guidance (Subhani, n.d.).

The essence of Islam lies in complete submission to Allah's will. True friendship entails prioritizing a friend's opinion over one's own in disagreements, but true faith involves placing Allah's commands above personal desires. Placing one's desires above divine guidance indicates a lack of genuine submission.

The examples of the Tribe of Thaqif and particular companions during Hajj underscore the principle of prioritizing divine commands. Some companions hesitated to come out of Ihram despite the Prophet's instructions, revealing a lack of submission. The verse serves as a reminder to believers to submit wholly to Allah and His Messenger's teachings.

In conclusion, the verse admonishes believers to prioritize Allah's commands over personal opinions, maintaining true submission to His will. The history of Islam offers valuable lessons on the consequences of disregarding this principle, urging believers to embrace complete obedience and submission to divine guidance.

# The Role of Faith

As it is written in the Bible, "Faith shows the reality of what we hope for; it is the evidence of things we cannot see" (*New International Version,* 2011/1973, Hebrews 11:1).

Faith holds a central place in the Christian life, and the Bible provides a definitive perspective on its nature and significance. The concept of faith is multifaceted and often understood differently in various contexts. In the world, faith might be seen as belief without tangible proof, while in spirituality, especially within Christianity, it is rooted in a confident trust in God based on His revealed Word.

Although its authorship is debated, the book of Hebrews holds authoritative status in the Bible and offers a profound definition of faith. It describes faith as the assurance of things hoped for and the conviction of things not seen. This definition emphasizes believers' confident trust in God's promises and His unseen realities.

The source of the Christian faith is God's unerring and rich Word, as found in the Holy Bible. Unlike the worldly notion of faith, which might lack evidence, Christian faith is founded on the reliable and unwavering truths communicated through scripture. This faith is not blind or irrational; it is rational and grounded in the revealed truth of God's character, actions, and promises (Cortez, 2018).

The process of receiving faith involves hearing the message of Christ, as highlighted in Romans 10:17, which says that faith is cultivated through exposure to the Word of God and the Gospel, leading to a deepening trust in God's redemptive plan through Jesus Christ (*New International Version,* 2011/1973, Romans 10:17).

From the Christian perspective, faith goes beyond mere intellectual assent. It involves a heart transformation that results in loving obedience and a desire to live out the truth of God's Word. This faith prompts believers to act in accordance with their trust in God, leading to good works that are motivated by love and devotion.

Ultimately, faith plays a vital role in the Christian journey, serving as the bedrock of trust in God's promises and the unseen realities of His kingdom. It shapes beliefs, attitudes, and actions, driving believers to live out their convictions and obey God's will.

## From Belief to Faith

Judaism uniquely embraces skeptics within its community. Judaism doesn't demand this, unlike some religions, which require explicit faith declarations. Doubt and uncertainty are seen as catalysts for spiritual growth. The Torah even celebrates skepticism. Unlike rigid beliefs in other faiths, Judaism values diverse thought and doesn't rely on unwavering certainty (Gordis, 2019).

Though belief in God is integral, Judaism provides limited outlets for open pondering. This absence can isolate those seeking reassurance about uncertainties. While figures like Maimonides advocated structured beliefs, Judaism recognizes varied reactions to the world. It accommodates skeptics by not demanding rigid theological conviction.

Judaism takes doubts seriously, acknowledging that spiritual journeys often start in confusion. It values experiences triggering introspection.

Contrary to common conversations about belief, Judaism focuses on experiencing God's presence rather than proving existence.

In essence, Judaism's approach to skepticism values inquiries, appreciates doubt's role, and provides space for exploring beliefs and experiencing the Almighty.

## Definition of Faith in Islam

Understanding the essence of faith in Islam is crucial, as misconceptions have caused historical issues. Early Muslims held a clear concept of faith, pivotal for our comprehension. In Arabic, "faith" (*al-iman*) combines affirmation and compliance, as Ibn Taymiyyah clarifies: "Faith affirms words of the heart, belief, and actions of the heart, compliance" (*Importance of reflection*, 2017).

Faith in Islam entails believing in Allah, affirming His truth, and obeying. The six pillars of faith involve Allah, angels, messengers, books, Judgment Day, and providence. The Quran instructs believers in these aspects. The Prophet Muhammad stated faith involves these six pillars.

True faith is beyond belief; Satan believes but lacks faith due to arrogance. Faith isn't blind acceptance; Allah's signs infer His existence. Islam's faith integrates heart, speech, and actions. It avoids extremes, affirming deeds, and beliefs. Strong faith corresponds to quality deeds.

The Islamic faith comprises belief, affirmation, compliance with pillars, integrating sincerity, speech, and actions. It balances between extremes, stressing righteous deeds and sincere belief.

# Practices of Self-Reflection

Reflecting on signs in the universe and Islamic teachings is a significant act of worship in Islam, encouraged by the Quran. It involves pondering over the creation of the heavens and Earth and acknowledging Allah's power and purpose. The Quran emphasizes reflecting on these signs to deepen faith and seek salvation.

The Quran highlights the importance of contemplating the universe's wonders and Allah's creation. This extends to self-reflection, recognizing the signs within oneself.

Islamic teachings also stress the importance of self-examination, as seen in al-Hashr 59:18. Umar's advice, "Take stock of yourselves before you are brought to account," highlights the need to assess one's deeds and intentions (*The Holy Quran,* 2016, 59:18).

However, reflection and self-examination shouldn't lead to despair. The goal is to increase obedience and good deeds, not lose hope. There's no need for elaborate rituals or specific times; any moment of solitude with Allah suffices.

Islam values pondering over creation and self, as guided by the Quran and its teachings. It's a form of worship that fosters spiritual growth, reinforces faith, and encourages righteous actions.

The three Abrahamic religions advocate incorporating daily self-reflection and mindfulness into one's educational journey. It encourages the reader to adopt an attitude of continuous learning, inviting regular assessment of personal actions and decisions.

Judaism also reiterates the relevance of Yom Kippur, a time of collective introspection and self-evaluation, as a model for incorporating mindful self-reflection into daily life.

Ultimately, there is an emphasis on the transformative potential of deep reflection, application, and prayer in shaping individuals' character and facilitating a meaningful lifelong learning and growth journey.

Spiritual development is an enduring voyage of discovering how to remain connected with the divine presence of God. Encountering Jesus is not the culmination but rather the initiation of an ongoing expedition toward increasingly resembling His character.

Integral to this journey is the essential task of honestly evaluating your life, identifying areas where transformation is required, and seeking that change through the influence of the Holy Spirit (Gordon-Michaeli, 2019). Self-examination is a potent instrument through which you can advance and encounter God in the inner depths of your heart.

While modern society might not naturally incline toward such introspection, it is a spiritual discipline capable of significantly enriching your rapport with God.

## Challenges and Tests

More than just a specific era in history, modernity has brought about profound changes in how we perceive and experience life, particularly in our understanding of religious traditions.

The removal of metaphorical and physical barriers, often called "ghetto walls," has placed Judaism in a competitive position within a diverse marketplace of ideas. The reliance on assumed

Jewish identity or anti-Semitism to foster a sense of belonging is no longer tenable. Instead, Jewish values must be re-examined and adapted to address modernity's myriad questions and realities (Harris, 2021).

The central challenge facing contemporary Jewry revolves around embracing modernity within the framework of Jewish identity and deciphering the implications of this embrace for the future of Jewish life. Scholars from the Shalom Hartman Institute have tackled three critical challenges brought about by modernity: the realm of ideas, the diversity challenge, and the challenge of statehood (Harris, 2021).

These writings provide insights into the direction Judaism could take in the future, offering perspectives on a range of topics, including the role of Israel in Jewish life, the collective identity of Jewish people, the interplay between monotheism and violence, and the intersections of Judaism with feminism and homosexuality (Harris, 2021).

Shifting gears to Christianity—there are three significant challenges it confronts today (Barton, 2013):

The ongoing issue of ecclesiology entails understanding the church's centrality within God's grand plan. The concept of redemption needs to be integrated into the broader context of God's purpose for the church.

The church's mission goes beyond making disciples and should align with God's overarching plan, encompassing more than mere outreach or teaching.

Christians engaging with and attempting to redeem culture must do so carefully to avoid becoming ensnared by worldly values.

For Muslim youth in the West, several challenges come to the fore. Firstly, navigating social activities without alcohol is possible and can be enjoyable. Secondly, finding the right balance between engaging with non-Muslim colleagues in social situations and maintaining one's religious values can be challenging.

Thirdly, understanding and adhering to Islamic principles while seeking a spouse can be complex, as unrealistic expectations and a shallow understanding of marriage can hinder the process (Mallery, 2022).

It's essential to recognize that these challenges are part of an ongoing journey of embracing and practicing one's faith in the modern world.

# Chapter 7:

# Moral Principles and Ethical Values

Across the Abrahamic religions, there exists a profound interconnectedness of shared moral principles and ethical values. This unites believers in their pursuit of virtuous and compassionate lives.

While specific rituals and practices may vary widely, these foundational values serve as guiding beacons, illuminating the path toward kindness, justice, humility, and empathy.

This chapter delves into the universal ethical threads that weave through different faiths, emphasizing the common ground upon which believers stand as they navigate the intricate web of human existence.

## Justice and Fairness

A recent study conducted by the Internal Revenue Service (IRS) has shed light on a concerning trend: The income gap has nearly doubled over the span of 25 years. Since the year 1980, a staggering discrepancy has emerged (Fiedler, 2011).

The stark reality is that while the incomes of 90% of Americans experienced a decline of nearly 1%, those at the upper echelons of wealth have seen their incomes grow by a significant 14% (Fiedler, 2011).

This economic inequality is not exclusive to one nation; it is a global phenomenon that manifests itself in various ways, including the proliferation of lavish mega-mansions in suburban areas and the continuation of substantial bonuses in the financial sector, especially on Wall Street.

This striking income disparity is not only a source of social instability but also raises profound ethical and religious questions, particularly in societies where Judaism, Christianity, and Islam hold significant sway.

Social justice stands as a central tenet in these prominent religious traditions. Its essence revolves around not only the fair allocation of resources within a society but also a profound sense of communal responsibility toward those in need and a moral imperative to empower the marginalized. This principle underscores the shared commitment within these faiths to actively address societal inequalities and promote a more just and compassionate world (Fiedler, 2011).

The foundational teachings of these faiths, which encapsulate the essence of social justice, have been voiced by revered figures such as Isaiah, Jeremiah, and Amos in Judaism, Jesus in Christianity, and the Prophet Mohammed in Islam.

These figures conveyed messages of fairness, compassion, and the imperative to address societal imbalances. The Jewish idea of *tikkun olam*, or "repairing the world," captures the heart of this mindset by pushing for proactive measures to bridge societal gaps (Fiedler, 2011).

The prophetic voices across these traditions have consistently championed justice. For instance, the Prophet Amos, who remains an influential figure even in modern times as evidenced by his frequent references by leaders like Martin Luther King Jr., passionately proclaimed the idea of justice flowing like a river and righteousness like an ever-flowing stream. In Christianity, the teachings of Jesus underline the centrality of justice, with his mission characterized as one of bringing good news to the poor. His memorable words, "Amen, I say to you, whatever you did for one of the least of these, you did it for me," underscore the imperative of caring for the marginalized and vulnerable (Fiedler, 2011).

Islam, often less discussed in the context of social justice, has an integral tradition known as zakat. This practice, one of the five pillars of Islam, requires Muslims to make an obligatory annual payment to be used for charitable and religious purposes. This practice directly aligns with the principles of social justice, promoting the sharing of wealth and resources with those in need.

Yet, despite the resonating voices of these religious leaders throughout history, contemporary societies continue to grapple with glaring inequalities. This raises pertinent questions about the prominence of justice-focused messages today. Do contemporary times lack the presence of visionary leaders and religious figures who are willing to fearlessly confront prevailing power structures and advocate for socio-economic fairness? When we examine the stark socio-economic inequalities of today, it prompts us to ponder the profound influence that prophetic voices of antiquity could wield if they were present in our current era (Fiedler, 2011).

These Abrahamic figures fearlessly denounced injustice in their times. They would undoubtedly do the same today, reminding us of our collective responsibility to pursue justice, compassion, and equality in our societies.

# Honesty and Integrity

The Quran states (*The Holy Quran*, 2016):

> And fulfil the covenant of Allah when you have made; and break not the oaths after making them firm, while you have made Allah your surety. Certainly, Allah knows what you do. And be not like unto her who, after having made it strong, breaks her yarn into pieces. You make your oaths a means of deceit between you, for fear lest one people become more powerful than another. Surely, Allah tries you therewith, and on the Day of Resurrection He will make clear to you that wherein you differed. (16:91)

This verse within the Holy Quran underscores the vital significance of upholding covenants and oaths made before Allah. The analogy of breaking yarn vividly portrays the seriousness of disregarding solemn promises. Beyond mere condemnation of deceptive oaths, the verse delves into the core essence of social justice. It cautions against exploiting agreements due to fears of power imbalances and advocates for fostering equitable relations.

This essential principle resonates deeply within Islamic teachings, placing a spotlight on values like integrity, honesty, and the sanctity of commitments. Adhering to oaths and contracts contributes to the cultivation of a just society, as Allah's omniscience enforces accountability. Furthermore, the verse serves as a litmus test for character, unveiling true intentions and the intricate interplay between faith and morality. It implies that ultimate clarity will emerge on the Day of Resurrection, offering resolutions to disputes stemming from broken promises, thus reinforcing the intrinsic connection between spirituality and the commitment to honoring one's word for the betterment of society.

In a world grappling with the erosion of honesty and integrity, the proliferation of deceptive schemes aimed at personal gain has reached concerning proportions. Unethical behaviors, spanning deceitfulness to unchecked greed, corrode trust and erode the foundations of ethical conduct. This disconcerting trend poses a challenge to societies, sparking concerns about the erosion of virtuous values.

"When a man vows a vow to the Lord, or swears an oath to bind himself by a pledge, he shall not break his word; he shall do according to all that proceeds from his mouth" (*The Torah*, 1996, Numbers 30:2).

Numbers 30:2 from the Torah, on the other hand, accentuates the sacredness of keeping one's word and upholding commitments. In an era where promises often remain unfulfilled, it accentuates the sanctity of vows made before the divine. It ardently advocates for the translation of spoken affirmations into tangible actions, nurturing trust within communities.

This guiding principle echoes prominently within Judaism, resonating as an ethical framework steering interpersonal relationships. Individuals who follow this guideline embrace a feeling of duty toward their fellow humans as well as the spiritual sphere. Numbers 30:2 remains an eternal reminder that words possess the potency to shape reality, with honoring commitments symbolizing a profound gesture toward reinforcing both human connections and divine principles.

The Book of Matthew states (*New International Version*, 2011/1973):

> You have heard that it was said to the men of old, "You shall not swear falsely, but shall perform to the Lord

what you have sworn." But I say to you, do not swear at all, either by heaven, for it is the throne of God, or by the earth, for it is his footstool, or by Jerusalem, for it is the city of the great King. And do not swear by your head, for you cannot make one hair white or black. Let what you say be simply "Yes" or "No"; anything more than this comes from evil. (Matthew 5:17–48)

In the Gospel of Matthew, particularly Matthew 5:33–37, we encounter Jesus's transformative ethical teachings on oaths and promises. Far surpassing adherence to traditional teachings, Jesus accentuates the values of integrity and honesty. He strongly discourages the act of making oaths, urging a communication style rooted in the authenticity and sanctity of creation. He underscores that elaborate oaths can introduce unnecessary complexities and insincerities, potentially paving the way for manipulation or deceit (*New International Version,* 2011/1973, Matthew 5:33–37).

This teaching calls for individuals to foster authenticity and transparency in interactions, nurturing a culture characterized by integrity and respect. Matthew 5:33–37 encapsulates Jesus's call for a profound transformation of the heart, urging a heightened ethical standard. It encourages a transition from formalities to a genuine, straightforward expression of truthfulness, consequently cultivating a community synonymous with trustworthiness.

In essence, these verses extracted from distinct religious texts underline the timeless significance of honesty, integrity, and the commitment to honoring one's word. They accentuate the pivotal nature of accountability, social justice, and the profound influence of words on personal character and the overall well-being of society.

# Respect for Life

The sacred teachings of Christianity, Islam, and Judaism, practiced by billions globally, interweave with the treatment of animals. In Christianity, the role of animals in sacrifices mirrors their importance in other faiths. Christians grapple with animal rights, prompting debates in countries like the United States and England. Peter Singer's work criticizes the Bible's dominion concept as hindering animal rights, yet diverse Christian views persist. While some see animals as resources, others stress kindness, considering harm to them sinful, revealing a nuanced interpretation of dominion (Kihlander, 2022).

Christian vegetarianism aligns faith with compassionate eating as awareness grows about food origins. Similarly, Islam, while endorsing animal use, deems cruelty a sin and prohibits nonfood killing. Islamic teachings emphasize mercy toward animals, equating their treatment with humans and condemning mental cruelty. Halal practices ensure humane slaughtering, although activists contest pre-stunning methods. Judaism underscores animal treatment due to their divine creation, forbidding cruelty. Yet, Judaism permits harm for human essential needs, recognizing human priority.

Gandhi's words echo across these traditions, highlighting the need for compassion. As religions evolve, the question arises whether animals' lives will gain further recognition within their religious contexts. Ultimately, Christianity, Islam, and Judaism align in considering animals as serving humanity, while emphasizing their kind treatment (Kihlander, 2022).

The interconnectedness of these faiths reverberates in their teachings, guiding believers' interactions with the animal kingdom and sparking ongoing dialogues about ethics, responsibility, and compassion.

## Humility and Humbleness

When considering humility, a spectrum of manifestations emerges spanning religious devotion, selfless charitable endeavors, and unassuming teamwork across domains like sports, business, and governance. Individuals may tailor daily actions to religious ideals, practicing gratitude and kindness. While numerous acts, such as public gratitude, accountability, and shunning the spotlight, are often seen as humble, they may merely reflect individual kindness rather than holistic humility.

Three prominent forms of humility surface: religious, public, and personal. Public humility, often perceived as contrived, finds expression in social media's "humblebrag" trend (APU Edge Staff, 2021). Yet, true humility tends to shy away from overt self-praise. Business humility surfaces when leaders tout humility's virtues, fostering a positive environment if genuine actions align with rhetoric. Recognizing authentic humility, like a true service mindset and sincere apologies, counters superficial displays.

Humble behavior thrives on the personal level, rooted in self-awareness and prioritizing others' needs without self-detriment. Genuine humility demands self-knowledge and a transformative life shift. It hinges on awareness, openness to feedback, and empathetic concern for others' well-being.

In pursuit of genuine humility, a wealth of resources exists, spanning books, essays, articles, and spiritual guidance. Yet, the crux lies in honest self-reflection and an embrace of diverse humility facets. Authenticity reigns supreme; avoiding insincerity and "humblebrags" is paramount.

In sum, humility's tapestry spans religions, workplaces, and personal interactions. It encompasses acts of kindness and profound introspection, all working harmoniously to create a world where selflessness and genuine respect reign.

## Forgiveness and Reconciliation

Various world religions emphasize the practice of forgiveness, rooted in love and purity of heart. Despite differing interpretations, the essence remains consistent across faiths.

Let's explore forgiveness within different religions (El Sayed, 2014).

In Judaism, the path to forgiveness involves a sincere apology from the wrongdoer. The wronged individual is religiously obliged to forgive, even in the absence of an apology. Forgiveness, deemed virtuous, is outlined in Deuteronomy 6:9. *Teshuvah*, meaning "returning," is a process of atonement involving cessation of harm, remorse, confession, and repentance. Yom Kippur, the Day of Atonement, holds special significance for Jews practicing *teshuvah*.

Christianity places forgiveness at the core of spiritual life, epitomized by the Lord's Prayer. Christ's dying words on the cross, "Father, forgive them, for they know not what they do," resonate as a timeless example (*New International Version*, 2011/1973, Luke 23:34). Unconditional forgiveness, love for enemies, and turning the other cheek exemplify Jesus's teachings.

Derived from "peace," Islam underscores forgiveness as essential for genuine peace. An excerpt from the Quran highlights the preference for forgiveness over retribution: "Although the just penalty for an injustice is an equivalent to retribution, those who pardon and maintain righteousness are rewarded by God. He does not love the unjust" (*The Holy Quran*, 2016, 42:40) The Forgiveness holds positive effects on well-being, maintaining social harmony, nurturing relationships, and promoting physical health. Beyond this, forgiveness liberates the human spirit.

In essence, forgiveness, a universal virtue, finds expression in different religious traditions, urging individuals to let go of grievances, embrace compassion, and foster inner and outer peace.

## Generosity and Charity

Kindness transcends religious boundaries, weaving through various faiths as a universal principle. It isn't solely reserved for times of crisis, but a perpetual pursuit rooted in belief systems. For instance, Islam places kindness at the heart of faith, with the Prophet emphasizing its significance. The pillars of Islam, from prayer to charity, cultivate inner kindness and empathy, driving actions like aiding bushfire relief efforts or assisting the elderly.

Judaism embraces charity, and the concept of giving is refined through the "ladder of giving." While donating to those in need is commendable, the highest level entails enabling self-sufficiency through education and training. Being a "mensch," exemplifying human virtues like kindness and righteousness, resonates within the Jewish tradition (Hegarty, 2020).

Christianity, fueled by the teachings of Jesus, underscores kindness and love. The sacrifice of Christ sets a benchmark for selflessness, encouraging believers to contemplate how they can sacrifice for others. Compassion is extended to all, even in simple acts like attentive listening to combat the modern loneliness epidemic. Charity becomes a joyful responsibility, rooted in the belief that generosity stems from divine guidance (Hegarty, 2020).

Presbyterian Pastor Mikey Tai practices daily kindness, prompted by Bible readings and prayer. The question, "What is a loving thing to do at this moment?" serves as a compass, ensuring kindness remains innate. Regardless of the faith, kindness is a common thread, binding individuals in a shared pursuit of bettering themselves and the world around them (Hegarty, 2020).

## Sincerity in Prayer and Worship

Prayer, at its core, requires sincerity devoid of hypocrisy or pretense. This authenticity is characterized by honesty, openness, and transparency. When we engage in genuine prayer, we lay bare our true feelings, withholding nothing. This earnestness is essential for nurturing a meaningful relationship with the Most High, as it invites reciprocation from God.

Outlined here are two ways to cultivate sincerity in prayer (Nielson, 2017):

1. **Cultivate forgiveness:** Unforgiveness obstructs our relationship with both God and others. The act of forgiving is pivotal, as harboring grudges alienates us from God and fosters self-deception. Unforgiveness erects walls, distancing us from both God and fellow

humans. It corrodes our ability to pray sincerely, leaving us consumed by bitterness, defensiveness, and self-justification. Shedding the weight of unforgiveness is vital for opening ourselves to authentic prayer.

2. **Embrace God's forgiveness:** Christ's sacrifice offers redemption from sin, granting us the courage to approach God openly. Confessing and repenting our sins invites His forgiveness and cleansing. This process restores our boldness to come before Him in prayer, once to seek forgiveness and later to present various requests. God's grace provides the boldness to be transparent in His presence, fostering a newfound love for sincere and unreserved prayer.

This cycle of boldness is fueled by ongoing confession and repentance, which continually renews the freedom to be candid before God. As we humbly seek His forgiveness, we experience a liberating transparency that fuels a deeper connection. Sincere prayer becomes a conduit for personal growth and an avenue to deepen our love for and relationship with the Almighty Father.

# Chapter 8:

# Community and Communal Worship

In a world as diverse as a garden in full bloom, the essence of a religious community stands tall like an ancient oak, its branches reaching out to touch the skies of unity. At its heart lies the sacred ember of communal worship—a flame that warms not just the individual soul but weaves a tapestry of shared spirit that connects us all.

Like the storytellers of old, history has etched its tales with gatherings where souls converged to dance with rituals, seek celestial wisdom, and forge bonds that transcend the bounds of belief.

Now, let us embark on this journey to plumb the depths of the sacred well of the religious community. Let us unfurl the scrolls that reveal how communal worship tends to the garden of our souls, nurturing growth and crafting shared tales.

As we traverse the labyrinth of devotion and collective devotion, we'll discover a truth as ancient as starlight. This truth resonates within our souls: The harmony of individuals within a religious community lends its enchantment to the symphony of human spirituality.

As the moon guides the tides and the sun paints the dawn, so does the dance of hearts and minds within these hallowed circles illuminate the grand design of our shared human quest for meaning and deliverance.

## Importance of Community

Religion has a complex role in shaping communities, both in terms of division and unity. While it can be a source of conflict, it has also played an important historical role in binding people together and fostering a sense of belonging. The term "religio," which means that which binds together, highlights the inherent nature of religion to create connections among individuals (*How religion strengthens,* 2020).

However, it's essential to explore whether the practices that strengthen specific religious communities also contribute to building more inclusive and diverse communities on a broader scale.

Personal experiences with religion vary widely, from casual adherence to fervent belief. Some individuals may have grown up in a family where religious practices were followed sporadically and without deep commitment. Despite this, there can still be moments of connection and affinity tied to religious spaces, such as churches, mosques, or synagogues.

These spaces become more about the shared experiences and milestones of the community rather than strict adherence to religious doctrines. In this way, religion serves as a thread that weaves people's lives together, marking significant events and changes.

The concept of "religion" goes beyond the conventional definition of faith in a higher power and holy texts. It encompasses shared values, rituals, and mutual respect for diverse beliefs. A strong sense of community can emerge not necessarily from religious beliefs themselves, but from the respectful coexistence of various religious and nonreligious perspectives (*How religion strengthens,* 2020).

The example of the U.S. military demonstrates that successful collaboration and cohesion can stem from a commitment to allowing differing practices and beliefs without imposing a dominant religion.

Another example is of an American man who grew up in a Catholic home. In his upbringing, he experienced the presence of religion in a nominally Catholic family, where church attendance was limited to significant life events such as baptisms, weddings, and funerals.

The rituals and practices of Catholicism played a role in his early years, marked by catechism classes that lacked a deep-rooted belief in God. As he progressed through his school years, a shift occurred, leading him to identify as an atheist by seventh grade. Subsequently, in high school, he embraced the Islamic faith.

Having now been a practicing Muslim for over 16 years, he found himself back at the family church for a wedding. An unexpected sentiment of genuine fondness welled up as he occupied the familiar pews. Memories of past baptisms, weddings, and funerals intertwined with the present, forging a connection to the church beyond theological beliefs.

Observing the congregation, he recognized faces from various life events, shaping the church into a symbol of shared experiences and familial journeys. It had transitioned from a place of theological significance to a space emblematic of the collective milestones and connections within his family. While his intellectual detachment from Catholic doctrine persisted, the church had evolved into a cherished location that encapsulated the family bond (*How religion strengthens,* 2020).

In today's diverse and interconnected world, acknowledging and respecting individual beliefs, or the absence thereof, is crucial for fostering harmonious communities.

Thus, while religion has historically been a binding force, the emphasis should not solely be on the faith itself. Instead, it should be on the values of tolerance, respect, and acceptance, which allow communities to thrive even amidst religious diversity.

The ability to coexist and appreciate different beliefs without imposing them on others is a key factor in building strong, inclusive, and harmonious communities.

## Communal Worship Practices

Worship, a profound expression of devotion, not only transcends the barriers of culture but also defies the constraints of time, extending its reach into the eternal. In the act of communal worship, believers of the present age catch fleeting glimpses of the boundless expanse of eternity.

Worship transcends the present moment, merging with the celestial symphony of angels and the host of heaven, whether it resonates in the reverent cadence of the Preface of the Service of the Sacrament, where we join ourselves "with angels and archangels and with all the company of heaven," or in the introspective solitude of Compline, where we humbly admit our sins "before the whole company of heaven" (Lewis, 2019).

The timeless wisdom passed down by prophets and apostles maintains its poignant relevance, reverberating through epochs and speaking to the exigencies of contemporary existence. Yet, the weekly congregation we partake in is merely a prologue to the grand narrative, a prelude to the cosmic banquet that awaits us.

Within the embrace of community worship, a profound reminder takes root in our hearts—the heavenly glory that beckons us forward, a promise of the divine feast that shall ultimately be our own. The Epistle to the Hebrews states, "Stir up one another to love and good works, not neglecting to meet together, as is the habit of some, but encouraging one another, and all the more as you see the Day drawing near" (Lewis, 2019).

Moreover, the Revelation of Saint John unveils a vision of "the continuing worship of God's people. The heavenly banquet is being prepared by Jesus, and He will return to bring us to celebrate with Him eternally" (Lewis, 2019).

As the final Benediction resounds on this terrestrial stage, the arras of worship extends into the dawn of a new creation. The enthroned Lamb will be loved in this celestial state by an orchestra of Psalms—victory songs harmoniously performed by God's beloved servants.

It is here, within the continuum of worship, that the universality of faith is illuminated. Islam, with its profound teachings and spiritual wisdom, stands alongside other faith traditions, threading a rich narrative of devotion.

Islamic traditions ring with prayers and prostrations, linking believers across the fabric of time and space, just as the calls of angels reverberate through the annals of devotion. The faithful, whether gathered in a mosque, a church, or any other sacred site, merge in their collective desire for the Most High in the embrace of community (Lewis, 2019).

In the expansive mosaic of worship, the devotion of the faithful transcends the divisions of earthly constructs and emerges as a testament to the unity of humanity's quest for the divine. This unity, built into the foundation of diverse faith traditions, bears witness to the eternal essence of worship—its ability to bridge cultures, traverse epochs, and illuminate the path toward the sublime.

## Festivals and Celebrations

Festivals and celebrations weave a sacred thread through the intricate fabric of religious practices, weaving together the spiritual lives of believers and cultivating a profound sense of unity and reverence. Across the landscapes of various faith traditions, from Judaism and Christianity to Islam, these cherished occasions serve as milestones, guiding the faithful on journeys of remembrance, reflection, and renewal.

In the realm of Judaism, the calendar dances to the rhythm of significant festivals, each resonating with echoes of history. Rosh Hashanah, the Jewish New Year festival, signals a time of introspection and renewal, inviting individuals to reflect upon their deeds and seek divine forgiveness. Yom Kippur, a solemn Day of Atonement, summons souls to partake in introspective prayer and fasting, a collective symphony of repentance and reconciliation.

Passover, a celebration of liberation, intertwines the past with the present, as families come together to recount the tale of Egypt's exodus, forging connections between generations and cultivating a shared narrative. Hanukkah, a festival of lights, kindles a beacon of hope, a reminder of resilience and the miraculous (*Judaism: Celebrations and festivals,* n.d.).

Christianity, too, is bedecked with a multiplicity of celebrations, paying homage to pivotal moments in the life of Jesus Christ.

Advent unfolds a period of anticipation and preparation as candles illuminate the path toward the Christ-child's birth. Lent, echoing the 40 days and 40 nights Jesus fasted and prayed in the desert, beckons the faithful to self-examination and spiritual discipline.

Easter, the radiant apex of the Christian calendar, resounds with the triumphant declaration of Christ's resurrection, a symphony that heralds the conquest of death and the unwavering pledge of everlasting life.

Pentecost, a glorious celebration of the Holy Spirit's descent upon the faithful disciples, stands as a radiant beacon, gently reminding the Christian community of the ever-present divine guidance and the endless wellspring of inspiration that courses through its collective heart (*Christianity: Celebrations and festivals,* n.d.).

In the embrace of Islam, devotion is intricately woven with festivals that honor the pillars of faith and nurture spiritual growth. Ramadan, a month of fasting and heightened worship, underscores self-discipline and empathy, fostering a deep connection with God and compassion for others.

Eid-ul-Fitr, a joyful crescendo of Ramadan, marks the breaking of the fast and the spirit of sharing. Eid-ul-Adha, the festival of sacrifice, commemorates Abraham's willingness to sacrifice his son as an act of obedience, emphasizing the values of submission and devotion.

Al-Hijra, the Islamic New Year, beckons believers to reflect on migration and renewal, bridging yesteryears with the present. Mawlid un Nabi, the celebration of the Prophet's birthday, serves as an occasion to honor his life and teachings, strengthening the bond between believers and their spiritual exemplar. Ashura, a day of fasting and contemplation, sings of purification and repentance.

Collectively, these festivals and celebrations transcend mere observance, serving as conduits for communal worship, spiritual growth, and cultural expression. They unite believers across time and space, fostering a profound sense of interconnectedness and shared purpose (Ismail, 2022).

As believers gather to honor these sacred moments, they partake in acts of devotion that not only tie them to their respective faiths but also interlace the vibrant threads of a harmonious global family.

## Spiritual Guidance and Leadership

Spiritual guidance and leadership play a profound role in nurturing peoples' holistic well-being and fostering a deeper connection to their faith and inner selves. Within the realm of healthcare, the concept of spiritual care has emerged as an integral component of comprehensive well-being (Puchalski, 1970).

Spiritual health holds a significant influence over a person's overall quality of life, with individuals experiencing spiritual distress often grappling with heightened levels of depression and anxiety. In light of this, clinicians are increasingly recognizing the importance of addressing patients' spiritual dimensions as an essential aspect of their comprehensive care.

Spiritual leaders embody multifaceted roles that encompass providing spiritual care, wisdom, and leadership. Analogous to skilled shepherds tending to their flock, these leaders offer compassionate care to those under their guidance, fostering an environment of trust and support.

Their insights and guidance serve as beacons of spiritual wisdom, illuminating the path toward greater understanding and connection with faith. Moreover, spiritual leaders assume the responsibility of spiritual leadership, overseeing and guiding the various aspects of their community's ministry, ensuring its harmonious and purposeful progression.

The power of sermons, teaching, and religious education cannot be overstated in their capacity to guide and inspire us along our spiritual journey. Through these mediums, we receive spiritual nourishment and intellectual stimulation, invigorating our quest for meaning and understanding.

Mentorship and discipleship emerge as transformative channels through which we can embark on a transformative journey toward deeper spiritual awareness. The essence of discipleship lies in guiding believers to embody the teachings of their faith and empowering them to share its wisdom with others.

This cyclic process cultivates a community of individuals who, in turn, become mentors, perpetuating the cycle of growth and enlightenment. On a more personalized level, mentorship hones in on specific areas of development, offering tailored guidance and expertise to aid a person's progress along their spiritual path.

Counseling and spiritual care manifest as essential facets of spiritual leadership, providing solace and guidance to those facing personal challenges and navigating moral dilemmas. The practice of spiritual therapy transcends conventional counseling by encompassing the realm of the soul and spirit.

Rooted in our unique belief systems and faith in a higher power, spiritual therapy delves into areas of inner conflict, offering a profound means of healing and growth (Spain, 2017).

Spiritual leaders, through their counseling and spiritual care, become pillars of strength during times of crisis, offering unwavering support and empathy to those grappling with grief or seeking to find clarity amidst life's complexity.

Spiritual guidance and leadership form a vital support system and offer compassion and enlightenment, guiding us toward a deeper connection with our faith, inner selves, and the broader community. Through their multifaceted roles, spiritual leaders serve as beacons of wisdom, mentors, and compassionate caregivers, nurturing a space where we can explore, grow, and flourish on our spiritual journey.

## Communal Ethics and Accountability

Empathy and compassion, revered as core virtues within Abrahamic faiths and secular societies alike, serve as potent catalysts for fostering mutual understanding among diverse ethnic and religious communities. These values, though rooted in various belief systems, transcend the boundaries of dogma and culture, functioning as essential tools in the delicate art of building trust across multifaceted divides.

Mutual understanding, nurtured by the twin forces of empathy and compassion, emerges as a vital conduit through which people can traverse the labyrinthine alleys of dissimilar backgrounds. As people begin to comprehend the joys, struggles, and aspirations of others, the boundaries of "us" and "them" gradually blur, giving rise to a shared human experience that transcends superficial differences (Oates, 2019). In the mosaic of diverse narratives, mutual understanding serves as the adhesive that binds these fragments into a coherent and harmonious whole.

This interconnectedness bears remarkable implications for bridge-building, the foundational infrastructure for fostering intercultural harmony and cooperation. Empathy, acting as a lens through which to perceive the world from another's vantage point, unlocks the doors to dialogue. It enables us to dismantle the barriers of prejudice, replacing them with bridges of respect and curiosity.

When paired with compassion, this exchange becomes a wellspring of shared wisdom, enabling the construction of bridges that span the realms of culture, faith, and tradition. These bridges, metaphoric expressions of human connection, span not only geographic divides but also ideological ones, facilitating the flow of understanding and nurturing an environment conducive to coexistence.

In the broader narrative of ethical conduct and social responsibility, empathy and compassion occupy pivotal roles. Ethical conduct emanates from an innate understanding of the impact of our actions on others, a trait heightened through empathetic awareness.

When individuals are able to place themselves in another's shoes, a profound sense of responsibility to act ethically and justly takes root. Compassion, in turn, fuels a deep commitment to alleviating suffering and injustice, driving us to actively engage in acts of social responsibility.

The symbiotic relationship between empathy, compassion, and ethical conduct extends further, culminating in the cultivation of social harmony. The nurturing of a society grounded in shared values of understanding, empathy, and compassion creates an environment where we are inherently attuned to the needs of our fellow human beings. This ethos of interconnectedness forms the bedrock of social responsibility, sparking a collective drive to address systemic inequalities, protect vulnerable populations, and champion the cause of justice.

By forging connections between Abrahamic faiths and secular norms through these shared virtues, the intricate web of intercultural tolerance is intricately woven. The intersections of empathy, compassion, ethical conduct, and social responsibility converge to create a realm where diversity is celebrated, and unity is fortified.

This shared platform not only promotes understanding but also inspires collaborative efforts toward building a society where compassion is not just a personal virtue but a collective creed.

In this grand web of human experience, empathy and compassion stand as the golden threads that sew together the fragments of our shared humanity, fostering an inclusive and harmonious mosaic of existence.

# Chapter 9:

# Social Justice and Moral Responsibility

Festivals and celebrations weave a sacred thread through the intricate fabric of religious practices, weaving together the spiritual lives of believers and cultivating a profound sense of unity and reverence.

## Advocacy for the Marginalized

Historically, Christians and Jews had shared relatively amicable relations until the 11th century, characterized by intermarriage, shared language, and culture. However, the dynamics shifted as Christian society underwent reorganization from the year 1000 onward, leading to the marginalization of various groups, including Jews (Cohen, n.d.).

During the early Middle Ages, interactions between Christians and Jews were frequent, and they even shared marital and cultural bonds. The era witnessed some Christian leaders expressing concerns that rulers excessively favored the Jews. However, the climate began to change after the 11th century, with Jews facing violent attacks and forced conversions in different parts of Europe.

This era also saw the emergence of anti-Semitic stereotypes and a deteriorating image of Jews among Christians. Tragic events like the blood libel accusations further strained relations. Concurrently, the church's official stance contributed to the declining position of Jews.

Pope Innocent III's decree of perpetual servitude for Jews and the Fourth Lateran Council's restrictions on their public activities underscored their marginalized status.

Economically, Jews were confined to money lending by the 12th and 13th centuries, contributing to animosity from borrowers and monarchs alike. The Jews' economic utility also led to a paradoxical relationship, as they provided capital to kings but were considered the king's personal property. This situation culminated in expulsions from various European countries, such as England in 1290 and Spain in 1492 (Cohen, n.d.).

Amid these challenges, conflicts and new movements arose within Jewish communities. Philosophical clashes between subcultures of Sephardic and Ashkenazic Jews revealed differing metaphysical doctrines seeking salvation through knowledge. However, ecclesiastical attacks on the Talmud and expulsions from France in 1306 prevented the resolution of these conflicts.

The 14th and 15th centuries witnessed increasing orthodoxy and uniformity of practice among the rabbinic circles, despite pockets of independent thought. The Spanish expulsion led to intensified pursuits of mystical escape and rationalization of the calamities befalling the Jews.

The upheaval spurred the establishment of a community in Zefat, Palestine, where saintliness and mystical contemplation were emphasized. The leaders sought to restore creation's harmony through liturgical innovation and mystical theology.

This period also saw attempts at ordination revival and the rise of dogmatic Kabbalism (Cohen, n.d.).

While the 18th century brought a decline in scholarship and a mechanization of popular religion, there was a restless search for new paths of faith beneath the surface. The century marked a turning point, with fresh responses that set Jewish history on new trajectories, opening the door to a new era.

Amidst the ebb and flow of political landscapes, theological discussions, and societal transformations, the medieval Jewish communities in Europe skillfully traversed an intricate landscape that left an indelible mark on their identity, customs, and connections with the broader Christian world.

## Muslims Marginalized in the United States

It's remarkable to learn that the United States is home to over 3 million Muslim Americans, mostly young adults. Islam's roots in America can be traced back over 400 years to the transatlantic slave trade era when many enslaved individuals from African countries who practiced Islam were brought to the U.S.

Today, Black Americans constitute the largest ethnic group among U.S. Muslims, and almost 90% of Muslims in America hold American citizenship, signifying their deep integration into the nation (Younus & Soto, 2021). This study highlights the profound bond between a strong Muslim identity and a deeply ingrained American identity, dispelling the notion that the two are inherently contradictory.

Muslim women within the American community perceive their faith as a source of joy and an integral component of their identity, instilling a deep sense of pride. Interestingly, women within the American Muslim community are recognized as one of the most educated female religious groups in the U.S. Although thirty percent of Muslims in America live in poverty, the Muslim community is commended for its charitable efforts, with charity donations from Muslims in Michigan totaling an impressive $117 million in 2015 (Younus & Soto, 2021).

However, philanthropic leaders lack awareness about the realities within the Muslim community, which poses a challenge when engaged in mission-related conversations. Marginalized communities face the additional hurdle of dispelling stereotypes before initiating meaningful discussions.

Nevertheless, Muslim leaders are taking steps to bridge the gap between their community and others by promoting understanding and support. For example, they were introduced to the Native Day of Learning by the Field Foundation, recognizing the potential for collective power and cooperation among marginalized communities. During a virtual launch event of "The Muslims in America: A Year of Learning for the Philanthropic Community," attendees had the chance to connect personally while gaining insights into Muslim culture through virtual experiences encompassing film, comedy, music, art, and history (Younus & Soto, 2021).

By emphasizing the importance of collaboration and inclusivity within philanthropic endeavors, this initiative underscores faith-inspired groups' vital role in providing social safety net services. Muslim leaders are committed to counteracting Islamophobic attitudes through well-organized initiatives and building a better, more inclusive society by supporting Muslim Americans' rich history and contributions.

# Peacemaking and Conflict Resolution

According to the Bible, humility is key to resolving conflicts. It advises us to be subject to our elders and to clothe ourselves with humility toward one another, for God opposes the proud but gives grace to the humble. While pride is a major issue, selfish motives can be just as dangerous. The New Testament explains that quarrels and fights stem from desires that wage war within us. These desires can lead to conflicts with anyone, from coworkers to family members (*Peacemaking 101*, 2021).

Conflict is a messy business, and many people try to avoid it altogether. However, Jesus encourages his followers not to put off addressing conflicts. In fact, reconciling with others is an essential part of reconciling with God. Often, pride is at the heart of many conflicts, and we must take a hard look at ourselves to ensure that it has no place within our hearts.

The Scripture provides guidance on how to resolve conflicts, with several verses supporting this process (*Peacemaking 101*, 2021):

- Seek to settle differences among yourselves (*New International Version*, 2011/1973, 2 Corinthians 13:11).

- Pause and aim for healing (*New International Version*, 2011/1973, Proverbs 12:18).

- Address your own shortcomings first (*New International Version*, 2011/1973, Matthew 7:5).

- Confront your brother or sister privately (*New International Version*, 2011/1973, Matthew 18:15–17).

God's objective aligns with his purpose in all things, which is restoration. Luke 17:3-4 reminds us of this, stating that if our brother sins, we should rebuke him, and if he repents, we should forgive him (*New International Version*, 2011/1973, Luke 17:3-4). Essentially, conflict resolution is a process of addressing disputes and fostering reconciliation and restoration, guided by humility, self-examination, and forgiveness (*Peacemaking 101*, 2021).

A vital step in conflict resolution emphasizes the importance of addressing conflicts directly with the person involved, either one-on-one or with a witness. If resolution remains elusive, the matter should escalate to a small group and, eventually, to the entire church or a conflict resolution committee. It's essential to understand that the ultimate goal of conflict resolution is not just about setting things right or proving a point.

## Opposition to Injustice

The teachings of Islam regarding justice are intricately linked with its theology, guiding believers to manifest divine attributes in their behavior and interactions, thereby fostering a society marked by fairness and equity.

In Islamic doctrine, justice is an inherent element of the universe's foundation. The Quran articulates, "God raised up the heavens and established the Scales of balance" (*The Holy Quran*, 2016, 4:158), which scholars interpret as an affirmation of the importance of "establishing justice." This notion of balance is central to the Islamic comprehension of justice, which involves upholding the rights owed to others.

At the core of this comprehension lies the concept of pure monotheism, acknowledging that God is the ultimate Sovereign and the sole object of worship. Any distortion of this monotheism, such as associating partners with God, is viewed as a grave injustice. Such distortions deprive individuals of spiritual fulfillment, subjecting them to false ideologies and worldly desires.

The Quran underscores this divine attribute with the declaration, "Verily, God does not do even an atom's weight of injustice" (*The Holy Quran*, 2016, 4:40). The Prophet Muhammad further conveys this divine principle by transmitting God's words, "O My Servants, I have forbidden injustice upon myself and have made it forbidden amongst you, so do not commit injustice" (Khan, 2020).

In this profound statement by the Prophet, a clear link emerges between human conduct and the recognition of God's divine attributes. Islamic theology emphasizes that our life's purpose is to draw nearer to God by reflecting His Divine Names and characteristics. This spiritual journey entails the cultivation of virtues within ourselves. The renowned theologian Abū Ḥāmid al-Ghazālī, in his treatise on the concept of God, elaborates on the idea that a worshiper's perfection and salvation are attained through emulating God's attributes to the extent humanly possible (Khan, 2020).

Every facet of life presents opportunities for us to embody virtues that mirror these divine qualities. Acts of compassion for the distressed, generosity toward the needy, and advocacy for the oppressed all stem from a commitment to justice. Belief in God's divine justice is inherently tied to the duty to strive for justice and to abstain from oppressing others.

Those who champion justice are deemed to possess a profound understanding of God's greatness: "God testifies that there is none worthy of worship except Him, as do the angels, and those endowed with knowledge standing firmly for justice" (*The*

*Holy Quran*, 2016, 3:18). In Islam, spiritual justice forms the bedrock of all other forms of justice.

A genuine connection with God is reflected in our interactions with others. Islam places immense emphasis on safeguarding the rights of all creations, from family and neighbors to humanity at large, animals, and the environment. The Quran highlights justice, upright behavior, care for relatives, and the prohibition of immorality, evil, and transgression.

Muslims are encouraged to approach every matter with justice and to uphold impartiality, even if it necessitates opposing their own interests. The Quran's wisdom advises, "Let not the hatred of others toward you prevent you from being just. Be just, that is closer to piety" (*The Holy Quran*, 2016, 5:8).

Islam categorically condemns all forms of racism, bigotry, and injustice. This fundamental principle finds its basis in both Quranic revelations and the teachings of the Prophet Muhammad.

The concept of justice in Islam is intricately entwined with the divine nature of God Himself.

## Poverty Alleviation

The fundamental concept of human dignity takes center stage in Judaism. The book of Genesis declares that humanity is fashioned in the likeness of God (*New International Version*, 2011/1973, Genesis 1:26). This belief underscores that any mistreatment of another human being is, at its core, a disregard for the divine. The term "achikha" reinforces the notion that every person, including the poor, is a manifestation of the divine image and should be treated accordingly.

The Jewish viewpoint concerning poverty and those in need is firmly rooted in the notion of human dignity, recognizing that every person, regardless of their economic standing, embodies the image of God. This perspective is encapsulated in the term "achikha" (your brother), signifying the importance of honoring the dignity of those facing poverty and urging individuals not to perceive them as fundamentally different or inferior.

Moreover, *achikha* serves as a reminder that we should not distance ourselves from the poor by finding reasons to differentiate between us and them. Often, people shield themselves from feelings of vulnerability by attributing poverty to perceived personal failings, such as laziness or poor choices. These barriers are dismantled by recognizing the poor as our siblings, and we are compelled to see past such judgments.

The Torah's reference to eradicating poverty while acknowledging its continued existence (*The Torah*, 1996, Deuteronomy 15:4, 11) may initially appear contradictory. This passage is often understood to reflect the tension between humanity's capacity to fully uphold commandments and the likelihood of lapses.

Traditional commentators suggest that the condition for poverty eradication relies on human obedience to commandments, an ideal that may not always be met. Rabbi Moshe ben Nachman Ramban offers an interpretation that combines optimism and realism.

He suggests that while periods of poverty may reoccur, the goal is to work toward a world without need. The Torah acknowledges that perfection may not always be attainable, yet it provides guidance for addressing poverty when it arises (Jacobs, 2021).

Judaism emphasizes everyone's inherent worth and promotes unity, compassion, and social responsibility. The term "achikha" embodies these values, encouraging the recognition of the poor as equals and underscoring the collective responsibility to address poverty and uphold human dignity.

## Global Responsibility

Personal responsibility being embraced necessitates the accurate placement of blame within one's own life. In the Bible, it is asserted that in matters of sin, only oneself can be blamed.

A direct result of one's own actions is every consequence that arises from sin. Whether one is struggling with anger, unforgiveness, lust, gossip, gluttony, idolatry, disrespect, or any other transgressions, the responsibility rests entirely upon the individual.

It's intriguing to note that the most significant obstacle faced by Israel was its own internal challenges. Even though they had witnessed divine interventions, including the miraculous parting of the Red Sea, the extraordinary provision of food in the wilderness, and the gift of a land they did not have to cultivate, along with cities they did not have to construct, their faith wavered, leading to their faltering. These remarkable manifestations of God's power should have instilled an unwavering confidence in His ability to conquer any adversity. However, the people's lack of faith ended up impeding the continuous flow of divine blessings and protection.

As we delve into the narratives of the Bible, a clear pattern emerges: the central cause of difficulties doesn't primarily stem from external adversaries such as the Philistines, Egyptians, Syrians, or Romans. Even formidable obstacles like the Red

Sea's impassable waters or the scarcity of essential resources like water and food failed to obstruct God's ultimate intentions for His people. Surprisingly, the most substantial hindrance to realizing His divine purpose frequently turned out to be the very individuals He sought to lead and guide (Ballenger, 2017).

Scripture emphasizes the need for accountability in personal sins. In instances of sin, there's often a tendency to seek alternative explanations for the wrongdoing. Factors such as family history of behaviors like anger or addiction, past traumas, or challenging environments may be pointed to.

However, the Bible maintains that the individual committing the sin remains responsible regardless of these contributing elements. It's crucial to recognize the true source of blame for sin; otherwise, seeking solutions will be misguided.

However, it's paramount to acknowledge that the ultimate solution rests in Jesus Christ. Relying on solutions other than Christ could lead to misplaced blame, even on God. Placing blame on external factors for sin could eventually culminate in holding God responsible when external changes don't eradicate sin.

Should we fail to take responsibility for our sins, Proverbs 19:3 highlights that our hearts may grow resentful toward the Lord. This essence of sin is effectively raging against God. The destructive path of attributing sin to external factors rather than acknowledging it as a product of one's sinful nature can greatly damage one's spiritual walk (Ballenger, 2017).

Rapidly repenting and accepting blame for our rebellion expedites the restoration of our relationship with God through His abundant grace and forgiveness. God doesn't require us to work to earn our salvation or attempt to alter every external trigger for sin. Instead, He invites us to admit our rebellion, repent, and rely on the transformative power of His grace through Jesus Christ.

Assuming personal responsibility for our failures leads to a deeper appreciation for God's grace and total redemption. Recognizing that we're fully accountable for our rebellion enhances our gratitude for God's complete forgiveness and eternal grace. This understanding forms the foundation of a heart full of thankfulness and devotion to God.

The Bible conveys that taking personal responsibility for oneself doesn't negate the need for Christ's solutions. Acknowledging personal inadequacy is a pivotal step toward God. While personal responsibility entails attributing blame for personal sins, it also entails seeking solutions in Christ's teachings. Despite God's sovereignty, assuming responsibility aligns with the biblical concept of personal accountability.

Recognizing personal accountability for actions and sins is central. It encourages acknowledging one's own faults, seeking God's forgiveness, and pursuing transformation through Christ. This approach leads to a humble and grateful relationship with God, rooted in understanding one's own limitations and Christ's redemptive grace.

Chapter 10:

# Bridging Differences Through Interfaith Dialogue

The importance of interfaith dialogue cannot be emphasized enough in its role of cultivating comprehension and cooperation among people hailing from diverse religious affiliations.

This practice fosters substantial conversations that result in mutual respect and a more profound understanding of varying perspectives. Interfaith dialogue deconstructs misunderstandings and forges connections between faiths by promoting open and respectful engagement.

Furthermore, this platform tackles shared challenges that transcend religious boundaries, including matters of social justice and the environment. Collaborative initiatives addressing these concerns bring together people from different faith backgrounds, creating positive changes at both local and global levels.

Interfaith dialogue's impact extends to nurturing empathy and compassion, key elements for peaceful coexistence in our interconnected world. By listening to each other's experiences, we personalize our understanding, promoting an environment of empathy and solidarity.

Additionally, this dialogue celebrates diversity while emphasizing universal human values shared across religions. Beyond distinctions, the core principles of compassion, justice, and kindness unite believers, enabling joint endeavors that go beyond religious divisions.

In a world often marred by misunderstandings, interfaith dialogue provides a constructive avenue for connection. It encourages unity amidst diversity, fostering harmony and inclusivity. Embracing interfaith dialogue propels us toward a more harmonious society where unity flourishes, and diversity is cherished.

## Importance of Interfaith Dialogue

Interfaith dialogue holds immense importance in today's globalized and diverse world. It plays a pivotal role in promoting understanding, tolerance, and cooperation among people of different religious beliefs. There are several reasons why interfaith dialogue is crucial.

It encourages us to engage in open and respectful conversations about our beliefs, practices, and values. This leads to a better understanding of other people's viewpoints and faiths, dispelling misconceptions and stereotypes. By facilitating conversations and interactions between religious communities, it contributes to peaceful coexistence. It helps prevent conflicts that can arise from misunderstandings and encourages the pursuit of common goals.

Through forthright discussions, we learn about the shared values and principles that underlie different faith traditions. This knowledge reduces prejudice and fosters a sense of unity among diverse groups. Interfaith dialogue creates bridges of connection between communities that might otherwise remain isolated. This connection can lead to collaborative efforts in addressing societal challenges.

Religious communities can work together through interfaith dialogue to address social issues like poverty, inequality, and environmental concerns. Joint efforts amplify the impact of these initiatives. Engaging in dialogue increases your knowledge about various religions, promoting religious literacy and cultural awareness. This knowledge contributes to a more informed and inclusive society.

It empowers us to confront our own biases and preconceived notions. It encourages personal growth and reflection. Dialogue provides a safe environment for discussing sensitive topics and asking questions. Participants can clarify misunderstandings and find common ground.

It also reinforces the importance of respecting each individual's right to religious freedom and encourages societies to uphold the rights of all religious minorities. By working together, people from different faiths can inspire positive change in their communities and beyond. This collective effort can lead to more just and compassionate societies.

In a world where diversity is increasing, and global challenges require collaboration, interfaith collaboration offers a path to harmony, understanding, and mutual respect among people of all faiths.

Matius Ho, Executive Director of the Leimena Institute, highlighted the potential of interfaith dialogue among the Abrahamic religions—as a means to acknowledge and respect shared values and differences (*Interfaith Dialogue,* 2020).

Dr. Alwi Shihab, Senior Fellow at the Leimena Institute, further emphasized the necessity of fostering deeper engagements among leaders from these three faiths. He proposed a program that facilitates the exchange of Abrahamic religious leaders between the United States and Indonesia as a means to stimulate more constructive dialogues for peace (*Interfaith Dialogue*, 2020).

Based in Washington, DC, the event featured other notable speakers and panelists. These included rabbis, Holocaust survivors, and congresspeople. The convergence of these influential voices underscores the commitment to fostering understanding and collaboration among Abrahamic faiths for a more peaceful world.

## Shared Beliefs and Values

The common ethical principles that various religious traditions share serve as a solid foundation for interfaith dialogue. These shared values provide a starting point for meaningful conversations and understanding among those from diverse religious backgrounds.

The concept of compassion, present in many religious teachings, emphasizes the importance of showing kindness and empathy toward all living beings. Whether it's the Christian principle of "loving thy neighbor," the Islamic principle of *rahma* (mercy), or the Jewish concept of *rachamim* (compassion), the emphasis on compassion bridges differences and encourages empathy (Gnosis, 2015).

Honesty and integrity are universally valued across religions. The ethical commitment to truthfulness and authenticity fosters trust among individuals and communities. This shared principle forms a basis for open and transparent dialogue.

The call for justice and fairness is a common thread among religious traditions. Maintaining the dignity and rights of all people, regardless of their beliefs, aligns with the core values of many faiths. This principle becomes a platform for addressing social inequalities and advocating for human rights.

The sanctity of life is emphasized in numerous religious teachings. Whether it's the reverence for life in Islam, the belief in the *imago dei* (image of God) in Christianity, or the interconnectedness of all life in Jewish spirituality, the value placed on life encourages a sense of shared responsibility for the well-being of the planet and its inhabitants.

These shared ethical principles transcend religious boundaries and offer a common ground for interfaith dialogue. When individuals from different faith backgrounds come together to discuss and uphold these values, they lay the groundwork for fostering mutual understanding, cooperation, and a more harmonious world.

At the core of this convergence lies the affirmation of the existence of a single God—the Absolute and Infinite Reality responsible for the ongoing creation and sustenance of all existence (Gnosis, 2015). It's crucial to acknowledge that these theological positions may undergo diverse interpretations within various branches of each faith.

Judaism, Christianity, and Islam share a substantial intersection in their theological beliefs and ethical values. These religions hold a common reverence for the figure of the prophet Abraham, forging stronger connections amongst themselves than with other belief systems.

This shared foundation establishes a sense of spiritual kinship between Jews, Christians, and Muslims. It's worth noting that this spiritual bond can be approached from various angles, as interpretations may differ.

Another significant factor contributing to the inherent affinity between these civilizations can be traced back to their shared roots in the monotheistic traditions of Islam, Christianity, and Judaism. All three religions trace their origins to a common ancestor—Abraham, a symbolic figure whose legacy endures in the city of Aleppo. It's noteworthy that Islam, as the most recent revelation among these religions, has consistently acknowledged and respected the older religious traditions.

This common ground not only emphasizes the spiritual and cultural ties between these civilizations but also dispels the notion of an inherent "clash of civilizations." Instead, it underscores the importance of combating ignorance through education and embracing diversity through pluralism.

Furthermore, it has offered successful cultural models, rooted in its diverse regional cultures, for the coexistence of different religious and ethnic groups.

# Interpreting Sacred Texts

Judaism, Christianity, and Islam find agreement on 18 out of the previously mentioned 28 theological stances. The first realm of concurrence revolves around theology itself, encompassing the unity of God, the concept of creation, the pre-existent Word of God, angels, human souls, the spiritual unity of humanity, divine revelations to prophets, the exemplar of Abraham, and the revelation of scriptures.

When examining their theological beliefs, divergences become apparent, especially concerning the status of Jesus. Judaism does not recognize Jesus as a prophet, whereas both Christianity and Islam acknowledge him as a prophet, messenger, and messiah, although they differ in their understanding of his divinity. Christianity views Jesus as the Son of God, part of the Holy Trinity, and God's incarnation on Earth. In contrast, Islam recognizes Muhammad as the final prophet and messenger of God, a distinction that Judaism and Christianity do not attribute to Muhammad.

Despite these theological distinctions, all three religions agree on the importance of adhering to divinely inspired laws such as the Torah, Halacha, Church Canon Law, and Shari'ah. These laws provide guidance for religious and societal activities, shaping the relationship between humans and God. Additionally, there are four shared theological positions between Christianity and Islam, totaling 22 shared beliefs. These include beliefs about Jesus, his predecessors, his virgin birth from Mary, and his role as God's prophet, messenger, and messiah (Christ) (Gnosis, 2015).

Beyond theology, there are shared practical aspects of daily life that hold significance across Judaism, Christianity, and Islam. These include the imperative of daily prayer, both formal and informal, as well as adherence to God's will through codes of conduct, shared values, and ethical principles. Other common beliefs encompass salvation through faith and divine grace, accountability on the Day of Judgment, and the aspiration for peace.

Despite theological disparities, the core understanding can be established through the acceptance of ethical principles that resonate among the Abrahamic faiths. While forms may differ, common ethical values permeate these faiths, guiding interactions with the marginalized and poor and societal issues in male-dominated environments.

This shared ethos prevails across Christian and Muslim cultures, highlighting the common ground despite theological distinctions. In light of these parallels, Jews, Christians, and Muslims, as descendants of Abraham, possess the capacity and responsibility to collaborate, leveraging their shared ethical foundation to elevate global society.

While it's acknowledged that religions can create divisions, today's imperative is to foster unity among diverse faiths to collectively address societal challenges. With a shared spiritual heritage as descendants of Abraham, there exists a call to address societal issues grounded in the same ethical framework.

## Exploring Theological Differences

The term "Abrahamic" is commonly used to encompass the Jewish, Christian, and Islamic faiths due to their shared connection to the patriarch Abraham.

The Jewish perspective on Abraham stems from the Book of Genesis. According to this tradition, Abraham left his father's land and settled in Canaan, encountering numerous adventures along the way. His wife Sarai, who later becomes Sarah, was initially barren.

To produce an heir, Sarah allowed her servant, Hagar, to conceive Ishmael. God promised them riches through their son Isaac.

Incorporating the Jewish account of Abraham, Christianity infuses it with theological significance. In the New Testament, Abraham's justification before God is attributed to his faith rather than solely his biological lineage and circumcision.

Conversely, the Islamic narrative distinguishes Abraham as the son of Azar, differentiating it from the Judeo-Christian version, which identifies his father as Terah. According to the Quran, Abraham received revelations from Allah and became a prophet who preached to his father, Azar, and others.

While there are differences in the narratives, Judaism, Christianity, and Islam, all agree that Abraham had both Sarah and Hagar as wives. In Islam, both Isaac and Ishmael are regarded as prophets, along with Lot, who preached to the people of Sodom and Gomorrah. Ishmael's descendants are believed to be the Arab people. The Quran recounts that Abraham and Ishmael were commanded to rebuild the Kaaba in Mecca, a sacred site for prostration and prayer.

Abraham is associated with numerous miracles, wisdom, and attributes of compassion. In the Quran, he is referred to as the "Khalil-Allah," meaning the "friend of God," a term also found in Hebrew and Christian Scriptures. While there are similarities in the narratives, differences exist. Christianity and Islam emphasize faith over biological lineage, a perspective traditional Judaism upholds. While Jews and Christians hold Abraham in high regard, his prophetic role varies between these traditions (*Differences and similarities*, 2012).

Respecting and understanding these differences is paramount. Acknowledging the variations and honoring diverse beliefs is more important than glossing over distinctions in an attempt to harmonize them.

# Seven Things Christians, Jews, and Muslims Share

Jesus Christ holds a significant place in Christianity and the Muslim faith, and it's worth noting his Jewish heritage. Here are seven lesser-known facts that connect the three major religions (Grün, 2014):

1. **Scriptural parallels:** These religions share similarities in their scriptures. Jewish holy texts comprise the Tanakh and the Talmud, with Christians adopting the Tanakh as the Old Testament. The Quran includes an account of Jesus' crucifixion, although Muslims view it as a spiritual event where God saved Jesus from his perceived fate.

2. **Shared holy city—Jerusalem:** The historical core of Jerusalem holds reverence for all three religions. Muslims consider the Dome of the Rock as sacred, marking the place from which Muhammad ascended to heaven. For Jews, Jerusalem is both a spiritual and ancestral home, while Christians regard it as the site of Jesus' burial and resurrection.

3. **Names for the divine:** "Allah" is the Arabic term for God, used by both Muslims and Arabic-speaking Christians. Christians and Jews also refer to God using specific names such as Elohim or Yahweh.

4. **Choral tradition:** The tradition of singing and chanting in religious practices, whether it's Gospel music in churches, synagogue chanting, or the Muslim call to prayer, has its roots in the need to reach worshippers, even those in the back pews.

5. **Interreligious prayer spaces:** With increasing secularization, finding places for worship can be challenging. Interreligious prayer rooms in spaces like airports, universities, and hospitals cater to believers of different faiths. These rooms encourage personal reflection and are designed neutrally, devoid of religious symbols, except for universally recognized emergency exit signs.

6. **Pilgrimage:** Mecca holds reverence as a destination for Muslim pilgrimages, while Jews and Christians undertake pilgrimages to Jerusalem.

7. **Abraham's unifying role:** Abraham plays a central role in uniting Christianity, Judaism, and Islam, earning these religions the title of Abrahamic faiths. He is considered the patriarch of the Jewish people and the founding father of the Arabic people. The Quran portrays Islam as a continuation of Abraham's original faith.

These lesser-known connections among Judaism, Christianity, and Islam demonstrate that common threads bind these religions together, even amidst their distinct beliefs and practices.

# Overcoming Stereotypes and Prejudice

To some extent, we all possess inherent prejudices as a natural aspect of human nature. Although these biases can assist in simplifying our perception of the world, they can also lead to negative interactions with others.

Fortunately, there are steps you can take to combat these biases effectively. Here's a three-step approach (*What can you*, 2020):

1. **Guard against biased behavior:** While harboring prejudices is a common human trait, it's essential not to let them dictate how you treat others. Never allow your biases to lead to exclusion or discrimination. Moreover, be mindful not to spread these biases to others. Strive to ensure that prejudiced thoughts do not guide your

actions, and actively work to treat all individuals fairly and respectfully.

2. **Acknowledge your prejudices:** The first and most crucial step in addressing everyday prejudices is recognizing and acknowledging their existence within yourself. It's important to understand that everyone holds preconceived notions about certain groups, even if these notions don't apply universally. Simply acknowledging this tendency is a significant leap forward.

3. **Take action:** When you encounter hurtful remarks, insults aimed at entire groups, or the reliance on prejudice to define individuals, don't hesitate to respond. Challenge such behavior! Whether it occurs within your circle of friends, on social media, or in other settings, you possess the power to make a difference. You can voice your disagreement, engage in constructive discussions, or employ various means to express your disapproval.

An extensive set of facts is not required to effectively counter prejudices, nor is expertise on every topic needed. In this endeavor, allies like common sense, empathy, and even humor can be utilized.

During discussions, the potency of asking questions can often surpass that of presenting facts or arguments. The revelation of inaccuracies or inconsistencies in certain statements can be made through consistent questioning, potentially leading to a reevaluation of the individual's stance. While immediate results may not be produced by this process, a gradual shift in perspective can be brought about over time.

By embracing these three straightforward steps, you can contribute to reducing prejudices in both yourself and others.

Take the initiative to learn about different cultures, religions, and backgrounds. Educate yourself through books, documentaries, online resources, and even direct conversations with individuals from diverse communities. This knowledge will enable you to challenge stereotypes and misconceptions, replacing ignorance with understanding.

Initiate conversations with people from different backgrounds, actively listening to their stories and perspectives. Engage in a dialogue that goes beyond surface-level differences and explores the common humanity that binds us. Ask open-ended questions and approach conversations with a genuine desire to learn.

Put yourself in others' shoes and strive to understand their experiences, challenges, and aspirations. Practicing empathy allows you to connect on a deeper level, acknowledging the shared emotions and struggles that transcend cultural and religious boundaries. As you cultivate empathy, you'll be better equipped to counter prejudice in yourself and foster understanding in others.

By taking these steps, you contribute to a more inclusive and accepting society, where prejudices are replaced by respect and genuine appreciation for the richness that diversity brings. Remember that change begins on an individual level, and your efforts can inspire others to join in the journey toward a more harmonious world.

## Chapter 11:

# Love and Compassion—

# Universal Spiritual Principles

The timeless spiritual principles of love and compassion run as a unifying thread across the teachings of Judaism, Christianity, and Islam. While these Abrahamic faiths hold distinct beliefs and practices, they share a profound agreement on the central role of love and compassion in shaping their doctrines.

In Judaism, the origins of love and compassion are intricately woven into the fabric of the Hebrew Scriptures, particularly within the Torah. The directive to love one's neighbor as oneself (*The Torah*, 1996, Leviticus 19:18) encapsulates the essence of extending kindness and understanding to others.

Within Christianity, love and compassion are not just integral but central to its teachings, epitomized by the life of Jesus Christ. The command to love one's neighbor and even extend that love to enemies (*New International Version,* 2011/1973, Matthew 5:44) underscores the revolutionary nature of Christian compassion.

In Islam, the teachings emphasize the vital significance of empathy and kindness toward every living being—whether it's humans, animals, or the environment. The exemplary conduct of the prophet Muhammad, who extended compassion to orphans, widows, and the marginalized, serves as a guiding light for Muslims, outlining a steadfast principle to be upheld.

# Love as the Core Principle

The Quran emphasizes that love is a divine attribute, as affirmed in verse 90 of Surah 11, where God is described as "All-merciful and Loving [wadud]" (*The Holy Quran*, 2016, 11:90). This concept is further reinforced by other divine attributes such as *Al Rahman* and *Al Rahim*, both stemming from the notion of *Al Rahma*, a distinct form of love. According to Sheikh Mohammad Ali Shomali, *Al Rahma* signifies proactive and selfless love (Farishta, 2020).

The Quran unveils multiple dimensions of Allah's love for His creations. The general love encompasses all of creation, irrespective of their deeds. This love extends even to wrongdoers, analogous to a mother's enduring affection for her child despite their flaws. A higher level of love is reserved for true believers who demonstrate trust and compliance with divine prescriptions. These individuals are "those whom He loves and who love Him" (*The Holy Quran*, 2016, 5:54).

God's love also extends to "the defenders of justice" (*The Holy Quran*, 2016, 5:42, 8:60), "those who purify themselves, the pious, those who trust Him" and "those who do good [to others]" (Farishta, 2020).

At the pinnacle is God's love for exceptional beings like the prophets. For instance, the prophet Muhammad holds titles like *Habib Ullah*, signifying the beloved of God, and *al-insan al-kamil*, denoting a perfected human being (Farishta, 2020).

However, this understanding of divine love differs from Christianity. While Islam acknowledges what God loves, it also underscores what He doesn't. This contrasts with the notion of unconditional divine love in Christianity (Farishta, 2020). Islam's approach aligns with the principle of divine justice, where beings are rewarded based on their actions.

There is a delicate balance between love and justice, which upholds human freedom and the importance of our actions. If divine love were entirely unconditional, the purpose of life might lose its significance. Within God's attributes, anger and mercy are interconnected and complementary. The concept of repentance further highlights God's boundless mercy. Despite His nonarbitrary love, God's compassion for wrongdoers exceeds expectations.

Unconditional love, when taken to an extreme, can compromise justice, much like a coach granting a football player the captain's position without considering their skills. Within God's mercy, there exist various facets of love, including anger and punishment. Parents, in their discipline, showcase profound love for their children as they guide them toward self-improvement.

The Quran also highlights the potential for repentance and transformation. God's proactive approach toward those who stray reiterates His initiative in restoring relationships. Repentance involves two divine interventions: enabling sincere repentance and forgiveness after repentance.

Human love for God is rooted in *fitrah*—an intrinsic nature that inclines toward beauty and perfection—attributes epitomized by God. The Quran affirms the priority of God in the lives of believers, with His love taking precedence above all else (*The Holy Quran*, 2016, 9:24). A hadith emphasizes the willingness of believers to submit to divine will and their practice of loving for divine contentment while disliking for His sake.

Within Islam, there is a strong emphasis on cultivating a pure and sincere love for the divine, which includes affection for that which aligns with God and aversion to anything opposing Him. This sentiment is mirrored by the concepts of "tavalli" (affection for things loving God) and "tabarri" (disapproval of realities rejecting Him), and it is exemplified by the stance of Prophet Abraham (*The Holy Quran*, 2016, 60:4).

Surpassing obligatory devotion, as per a prophetic hadith, leads to the awakening of God's love, fostering an intimate and mutual bond between humanity and the divine. In this relationship, believers seek proximity to God through their actions, and, in return, God reciprocates. This concept aligns with the idea of humans serving as God's vicars, entrusted with divine authority on Earth.

From the core teachings of Islam, offering believers a profound understanding of their relationship with the Creator, the concept of love, whether divine or human, is deeply intertwined.

## Divine Principles to Strengthen Your Relationships

God desires the utmost for us within the realm of life's intricacies. This extends to our connections with others, profoundly influenced by our faith. Reshaping our perspectives encompasses every facet, including how we engage with one another through surrendering to Christ's teachings.

Five paramount Christian principles underscore harmonious relationships, and embracing these principles leads to transformative shifts in how we connect.

The bedrock of meaningful connections lies in empathy and understanding, encapsulated in Proverbs 3:5–6. These principles call upon us to transcend the ego, embrace empathy, and actively seek comprehension in our relationships.

Joy is a divine aspiration for our connections, and through the Holy Spirit, we encounter both joy and peace, which in turn radiates hope (*New International Version,* 2011/1973, Romans 18:13). Additionally, Psalm 37:4 emphasizes the joy that arises from delighting in the Lord, infusing blessings into every aspect of life, including relationships (White, 2022).

Faithfulness, a virtue bestowed by the Holy Spirit, stands as another pillar governing our faith and relationships. Consistency, reliability, and devotion encapsulate faithfulness, mirroring the unchanging nature of God Himself. As God remains true to His promises, our commitment echoes in the faithfulness of our vows, especially within marriage.

Love, a cornerstone of Christianity, embodies selflessness and sacrifice. The ultimate act of divine love through the sacrifice of His Son sets the standard. This divine love prioritizes others' well-being over our own, urging us to embody it in our relationships.

Forgiveness, a challenging yet integral facet, lies at the heart of Christianity. Modeled by Jesus' crucifixion, it resonates deeply with our daily lives. Matthew 6:14 reinforces this, reminding us that our heavenly Father forgives us as we forgive others (*New International Version,* 2011/1973, Matthew 6:14). The choice to forgive influences the resilience or fragility of our relationships.

We coalesce efforts toward a more inclusive and accepting world by infusing these Christian principles into our relationships. The genesis of transformation lies within us, inspiring a ripple effect that encourages others on their journey toward a world illuminated by understanding and compassion.

# The Concept of Love for God

God's love for humanity might not be a common theme associated with Judaism, but it's an essential facet often overlooked. There's a prevalent misconception that Judaism is focused on strict judgment, unlike the New Testament's portrayal of God as love. However, this view is both inaccurate and harmful, perpetuating stereotypes.

It's crucial to understand that historical struggles and societal attitudes have shaped Judaism's rich tradition. Despite this, our past is filled with examples of embracing God's love. Rabbi Jonathan Sacks asserts that many Jews nowadays identify themselves through the eyes of Gentiles, which distorts our faith and diminishes our conviction in God's affection (Salkin, 2018).

In fact, Judaism has historically acknowledged and celebrated God's love. Early on, Jews saw themselves as beloved by God. The idea that the Old Testament depicts a judgmental God while the New Testament portrays a loving God is misguided. Judaism introduced the notion of a loving God, and this essence permeates the Bible.

The liturgy underscores this divine love, echoing sentiments such as "With a great love You have loved us; with eternal love You have loved us" (Salkin, 2018). Even in the Kiddush, the blessing over wine, we proclaim that God gifts us Shabbat with love. Abraham's selection by God exemplifies this love.

Judaism is, at its core, a remarkable love story. God and humanity's relationship follows stages akin to dating, courtship, and marriage. Just like any romantic connection, there are moments of disappointment, disagreements, and periods of silence. Yet, this love endures and evolves over time.

Our love for God is expressed through Torah study, which is like reading a love note. Mitzvot connects us to God's love, reminding us of His care. Loving each other and the world reflects our deep appreciation for God's love (Salkin, 2018).

Emanuel Levinas, a philosopher, highlighted that when we encounter others, we see God's image reflected, prompting us to embrace our duty to each other. This philosophy resonates with Judaism's fundamental belief in God's love for humanity and our role in manifesting that love through our interactions (Salkin, 2018).

The idea of God's love is intrinsic to Judaism yet often overshadowed by misunderstandings and historical traumas. It's time to reclaim this aspect of our faith and remember that, at its core, Judaism is founded on a deep and enduring love between God and humanity.

## The Importance of Self-Love

The concept of learning to love oneself has become so familiar that it often fades into the background noise of everyday conversations. It's like the repeated instruction from a parent to eat vegetables during childhood—a phrase that passes through one ear and out the other. However, the truth remains: Cultivating self-love holds immense significance.

An analogy that resonates with the process of self-love is that of the safety demonstration on an airplane. Flight attendants emphasize the significance of putting on your own oxygen mask before aiding others before departure. This is because if you don't ensure your own well-being, you won't be in a position to help anyone else.

This principle applies to self-love as well. If you're unable to provide yourself with the love and care you deserve, how can you extend it to others? For many, the absence of proper love during childhood and later in life makes learning self-love challenging. If you haven't experienced the love you needed in your formative years, it's not always easy to teach yourself how to love yourself.

Sometimes, allowing others to love you until you internalize self-love can be effective. Similarly, opening your heart to the love of a higher power, such as God, is a crucial step.

Brené Brown, a renowned author, emphasizes the significance of vulnerability and self-love. Loving oneself goes beyond mere feelings—it encompasses various aspects of life. Brown highlights setting boundaries as an act of self-love, stating that setting limits requires the strength to love oneself even when it means disappointing others (Seattle Christian, 2019).

Establishing firm boundaries is a way to express self-love. Many struggle with "people-pleasing" and setting boundaries, a challenge I have faced myself. Standing up for your beliefs, values, and what feels right or wrong is an act of self-love. Personally, I've learned to set boundaries and prioritize what aligns with my well-being.

Learning to love yourself unconditionally is demanding. This means embracing your body, mind, and soul—every facet of your being. Loving your body can be particularly challenging in a society that idealizes a certain appearance. Countless dollars are spent on advertising an unrealistic "ideal" body image. If you don't fit this mold, societal pressures can take a toll.

The media bombards us with messages dictating that we shouldn't have wrinkles, need a certain body type, or must adhere to specific beauty standards. Negative self-talk about our appearance becomes prevalent (Seattle Christian, 2019).

Quieting this external chatter and accepting yourself as you were created to be is vital. Embrace the idea that there's no universal definition of perfection. Each individual is unique and, importantly, made in the image of the Higher Power.

Reprogramming your inner dialogue to affirm your beauty and perfection, regardless of appearance, is a critical step. It's not an easy path to walk, but initiating a positive self-dialogue is a starting point. Shed the self-judgment and replace it with self-love.

## Kindness and Acts of Mercy

The prophet Muhammad exemplified love, kindness, and compassion through his interactions and teachings. His behavior displayed a remarkable level of care and tenderness, making him a role model for these virtues (Zohery, 2022).

The prophet consistently demonstrated acts of compassion, particularly toward vulnerable and marginalized individuals. Anas, who served him for 10 years, attested that he was never subjected to criticism or reprimand. Instead, the prophet's demeanor was consistently kind and understanding.

His compassion extended beyond personal relationships. He advised his wife, Aisha, to be charitable and considerate toward those in need, highlighting the importance of caring for the less fortunate. Furthermore, he encouraged a sense of community and solidarity by suggesting that help and sustenance are often facilitated through those who are considered weak or vulnerable.

Prophet Muhammad's conduct mirrored the compassionate nature of Allah, as he consistently displayed kindness toward all beings, regardless of their background or beliefs. He underscored the significance of kindness in various aspects of life, emphasizing that benevolence is a commendable trait in every situation.

Despite facing rejection and challenges from his own community, the prophet remained steadfast in his concern for their spiritual well-being. This genuine care for their guidance was an expression of his deep compassion.

His empathy extended to all humanity. His kindness was not confined to specific relationships; he advocated for treating friends, relatives, neighbors, and even strangers with kindness.

He emphasized the value of maintaining good relations with family and neighbors, thereby fostering a sense of interconnectedness and mutual support. Additionally, he stressed the importance of treating orphans kindly, underscoring the significance of their welfare.

The prophet's teachings encompassed the dignified treatment of women. He advocated for respect and fair treatment, discouraging any form of mistreatment. His emphasis on kindness toward women reflected his commitment to upholding their rights and well-being.

Beyond human beings, Muhammad extended his compassion to all living things. He advocated for humane treatment and emphasized that acts of kindness should extend to all living creatures. He encouraged responsible and considerate behavior toward animals, highlighting the interconnectedness of all life forms.

His life demonstrated an unwavering commitment to love, kindness, and compassion. His actions and teachings provided a blueprint for cultivating empathy and care toward all beings, promoting a harmonious and compassionate society.

# Compassion for Others

Emphasizing the paramount commandment, Jesus stressed the importance of wholeheartedly loving God. This was closely followed by His instruction to love one's neighbor as oneself. When asked about the single greatest commandment, Jesus introduced two closely linked principles guiding our actions and attitudes.

Naturally, loving our neighbors as we do ourselves originates from our devotion to God. As the Son of God, Jesus Christ mirrored the attributes of His Father, particularly compassion. A poignant instance of Jesus displaying compassion occurred when He witnessed His friends mourning the death of Lazarus. Deeply moved by their grief, He wept alongside them. His compassionate nature was also evident in His healing of large crowds who sought His presence and individuals in need of healing. Recognizing the spiritual hunger of the people, Jesus assumed the role of the true high priest, teaching them. This starkly contrasted with the neglectful religious leaders of that era who lacked compassion for the masses.

Within the Bible, the terms translated as "compassion" in both Hebrew and Greek convey the notions of showing mercy, experiencing sympathy, and feeling pity. It is well-established that Yahweh is characterized as a compassionate and merciful deity, exemplified by His attributes of love, faithfulness, and patience. Yahweh's compassion is unending and everlasting, with His mercies being renewed each day.

The apostle John raised a critical question concerning compassion in 1 John 3:17, highlighting that if someone possesses material resources and witnesses a brother in need without displaying compassion, their professed love for God comes into question (*New International Version*, 2011/1973, 1

John 3:17). This underscores the expectation for humanity, created in God's image, to reflect His attributes, including compassion. Similarly, St. John the Apostle emphasized the importance of loving one's brother as integral to loving God. The absence of compassion for others contradicts a proclaimed love for God (*What Does the Bible Say*, 2011).

The Bible establishes compassion as a core attribute of both God and His followers. This compassion is characterized by mercy, sympathy, and empathy and is demonstrated through actions that show kindness and understanding toward others.

# Chapter 12:

# Divine Guidance and Personal Discernment

Embarking on a spiritual journey means navigating the crossroads where religious teachings and personal discernment intersect. This juncture becomes a blend of ancient wisdom and individual insight, shaping the choices made along the path.

Religious teachings act as beacons, offering guidance and ethical frameworks honed over generations. They provide a foundation for understanding the world and our role in it. Yet, they're not fixed directives; instead, they offer room for interpretation and personal connection.

Amid these teachings, personal discernment arises as a precious skill. It's the echo of our life experiences and inner truths. This inner voice emerges from stillness and contemplation, guiding us toward choices that resonate with our deepest selves.

Balancing this duality is a thoughtful process. It involves studying scriptures and traditions and seeking counsel from mentors. However, it's equally about quieting the mind to hear the murmurs of our inner beings. It's about fusing our choices with the essence of faith and personal authenticity.

This is not about choosing one aspect over the other: It's about harmonizing them. Religious teachings and personal discernment meld, enhancing each other's impact. When faced with decisions, we draw from both wellsprings, honoring tradition while acknowledging our unique life path.

## Seeking Guidance From Sacred Texts

Sacred texts, revered as beacons of divine guidance, often prove elusive in their understanding, failing to lead individuals toward religion even after meticulous reading and analysis. This complex phenomenon intertwines elements of intention, heart condition, and receptivity to the divine message.

The purity of the heart yields profound influence over how effectively one absorbs the guidance embedded within sacred scriptures. It is the intention harbored within that ultimately determines whether a sacred text transcends being a mere historical record and becomes a guiding light.

Sacred passages resonate most with individuals whose hearts are characterized by humility, receptivity, and a genuine yearning for guidance. These texts possess the power to illuminate the minds of those who earnestly seek the truth and are open to its transformative impact.

Scriptures direct their light toward hearts that are receptive to belief and attuned to obedience to the Divine will. The presence of God-consciousness signifies a heart that is inherently receptive to the profound influence of Scripture. The guidance contained within these texts flows most profoundly to those who have aligned themselves with the divine and are willing vessels for its teachings.

In times of adversity, many of us naturally turn to God, finding solace, mercy, and direction within sacred texts. This is particularly true for those grappling with shattered spirits and yearning for redemption. The Word of God emerges as a luminous beacon guiding us back to the Creator, providing a sense of purpose and guidance in the face of life's challenges.

As people progress in their spiritual journey, there arises a yearning to directly comprehend the language of the divine. The realization dawns that human translations serve as intermediaries, prompting a desire to delve into the original texts for a deeper understanding of their essence and nuances.

Amidst this pursuit, it is essential to be vigilant against the devil's cunning schemes aimed at distorting the meanings of the Scriptures. Satan targets those deeply engaged in religious pursuits, weaving misleading interpretations and fostering time-consuming disputes. It is crucial to steer clear of unverified interpretations, innovations, and debates that lead to no fruitful outcome.

To unlock the essence of Abrahamic Scriptures, it is recommended to uphold one's belief, engage in knowledge-sharing circles, engage in private reflection upon its verses, and distance yourself from misleading influences.

Throughout this mission, mainstream religious scholarship serves as a safeguard, preserving the integrity of the Scripture. Navigating this path requires unwavering faith, constant introspection, and a conscious avoidance of anti-religious propaganda that could lead one astray.

The depths of the Torah, Bible, and Quran are unveiled when intentions align, hearts remain receptive, and souls yearn for truth. Their guidance flourishes within those who maintain a conscious awareness of the Almighty, coupled with steadfast faith and astute discernment.

It is vital to uphold the sanctity of sacred texts, guarding them against manipulation and allowing them to serve as guiding stars toward a deeper and more profound connection with the Holiest.

## Prayer as a Channel for Guidance

Prayer, serving as a universal cornerstone, stands as a unifying force among the Abrahamic faiths—Judaism, Christianity, and Islam—by offering a pathway for direct communication, spiritual guidance, and enlightenment from the Most High.

While each of these faiths encompasses unique rituals and practices, they share a common belief in the profound potential of prayer to establish a deep and meaningful connection with the Creator. It enables us to navigate the complexities of life with faith and purpose.

In the realm of Judaism, prayer is not an isolated practice but rather an integral thread woven into the fabric of daily existence. It functions as a means through which believers engage in ongoing conversations with God, expressing their innermost thoughts, emotions, and desires.

The narratives woven throughout the Hebrew Bible, such as Abraham's fervent plea for a son and Moses' quest for guidance during the Exodus, serve as vivid illustrations of seeking Divine direction through prayer.

Within the Jewish tradition, prayer becomes a powerful tool for aligning oneself with God's will, particularly in times of uncertainty and the pursuit of clarity.

Christianity, too, holds prayer in high regard, considering it an intimate and direct form of dialogue with the Lord. Instances from the Bible, such as Jesus' deeply contemplative prayer in the Garden of Gethsemane prior to his crucifixion, underscore the significance of seeking divine guidance and fostering communion through prayer.

Yet, prayer in Christianity transcends mere communication, as it taps into the wisdom of the Holy Spirit. This allows the faithful to discern God's plan and handle the problems that life throws at them with spiritual clarity and purpose.

Islam, on the other hand, elevates prayer to a central pillar of its faith, as evidenced by its inclusion as one of the Five Pillars that symbolize devotion to Allah. Muslims engage in prayer five times daily, creating a continuous and unwavering connection with the divine.

This practice is characterized by its structured nature, fostering an ongoing dialogue with God. The Quran itself features stories of those who turned to prayer in their quest for direction, with the prophet Muhammad's experiences during revelations serving as a significant example.

Islamic prayers are not only a means of communication but also a method to seek divine guidance and a source of spiritual nourishment.

Ultimately, the Abrahamic faiths converge in their shared belief that prayer serves as a potent conduit for seeking divinely inspired guidance and establishing a profound connection with the Creator.

Through the act of prayer, believers transcend the limitations of the earthly realm and access a dimension of insight, clarity, and direction. In these moments of communion with our Maker, we find solace, guidance, and a renewed sense of purpose in our respective faith journeys.

The act of prayer unites the Abrahamic faiths, providing believers with a universal method to connect with God and navigate the complexities of life with faith, hope, and a sense of spiritual direction.

## Meditative Practices

It is truly unfortunate how the discord among the Abrahamic religious traditions is often emphasized by news programs rather than their shared attributes. Several intricate factors can be attributed to this inclination to spotlight divisions over unity. A primary cause is the limited prevalence of religious literacy. Childhood is the period when religious education occurs, and it often concludes prematurely, leading to a restricted comprehension of our own beliefs and even less understanding of others' faiths. Frequently, the impression that our faith is right, while others are misguided, is inadvertently conveyed by religious education.

Additionally, the negative aspects of religious traditions, including extremism and harmful behavior, are frequently accentuated by the media. Positive news rarely captures attention (Plante, 2009). This unfortunate situation leaves many well-educated individuals with minimal knowledge about their own religion, and their perception of other faiths is often shaped by adverse news rather than accurate insights into their customs and convictions.

Contemplative practices, such as meditation, are frequently associated with Eastern traditions like yoga and mindfulness, while the profound meditative practices within Judaism, Christianity, and Islam often go unnoticed. However, valuable contemplative techniques that can enhance well-being, wisdom, and healing are also provided by these religions. A recent conference at Santa Clara University convened experts from various faiths to explore how diverse contemplative practices contribute to stress management, health, and healing (Plante, 2009).

While each religious tradition boasts distinct characteristics, it is worthwhile to acknowledge and value their contemplative methods. Similar to diverse cuisines offering various flavors, unique yet equally valuable advantages are offered by distinct contemplative practices. It is essential to recognize that not all traditions and practices are identical. While some adherents commit atrocious acts in the name of their faith, the majority are well-intentioned and compassionate. It is crucial to avoid making sweeping generalizations.

A constructive approach involves showing respect for and appreciating the contemplative practices of all traditions, while recognizing the goodness within these communities. While personal inclinations may lead one to gravitate toward the practices of a particular tradition, the contributions of various traditions to one's own experience and understanding can be enriched by appreciation.

Accessing the depth and richness offered by religious and spiritual traditions is possible by engaging with diverse practices and gaining knowledge about other faiths. Recent research and clinical practices support the notion that these practices positively contribute to well-being and health.

## Spiritual Mentors and Guides

Having a spiritual teacher and mentor is essential for maximizing your soul's potential in divine service. There are several reasons why this guidance is valuable (Silberberg, 2012):

- **Spiritual growth through guidance:** A mentor isn't just a friend offering help; they possess a deeper understanding of your spiritual journey. Their insights and teachings can facilitate profound transformation and growth in your relationship with the Most High.

- **Dual nature of the soul:** There is an existing idea that we have two souls within us—the animal soul driven by self-centered desires and the righteous soul propelled by a selfless connection with the Almighty. When two people seek spiritual growth together, the combined force of their righteous souls can overpower the influence of their animal souls.

- **Objective self-examination:** The sages highlight that it's challenging for individuals to objectively assess their own weaknesses and strengths. A mentor who knows us well can provide an impartial perspective, helping us identify our strengths and address our weaknesses, enabling growth in our spiritual journey.

- **Avoiding embarrassment:** Learning is hindered when one is too embarrassed to ask questions. Having a mentor fosters an open environment where one can freely discuss concerns and seek guidance without hesitation.

- **Wisdom of experience:** A mentor possesses the wisdom gained from their own experiences, making their guidance more effective and insightful. Their understanding of human struggles and spiritual development allows them to provide tailored advice and support.

- **External help in overcoming obstacles:** Similar to a prisoner needing external assistance to escape confinement, a mentor aids us in breaking free from the limitations imposed by our own negative inclinations. They offer guidance, wisdom, and support to lift us from the constraints of our destructive tendencies.

In essence, a spiritual mentor is a guide who assists you in navigating the complexities of your spiritual path. They offer a unique perspective, experience-based wisdom, and a nurturing environment that supports your soul's growth and connection to the Almighty. The mentor-student relationship is a cherished opportunity to learn, evolve, and draw closer to your spiritual goals.

## Scriptural Mentorship

The concept of spiritual mentorship is deeply rooted in the Bible, even though the term "mentor" might not be explicitly used. Throughout the Scriptures, we find examples of those who served as mentors, guiding and teaching others in their spiritual journeys (Peach, n.d.).

The most prominent example is that of Jesus Christ and His disciples, where the relationship between the Master and His followers embodies the essence of spiritual mentorship. As the disciples learned from Jesus, they later became mentors to others, passing on the teachings and principles they had learned.

Spiritual mentoring is distinct from traditional apprenticeships in that it involves modeling a mature Christian life and providing guidance to new believers as they navigate their faith. A spiritual mentor should strive to live a Christian life but doesn't need to be perfect.

Several principles gleaned from the Bible highlight the role of a spiritual mentor (Peach, n.d.):

- **Teaching and imparting knowledge:** A mentor serves as a teacher, imparting foundational truths and doctrines of the Abrahamic faith. This teaching goes beyond mere instruction; it involves jointly discovering answers to questions and seeking to understand the Word of God. The mentor need not be an expert but should be equipped to answer basic questions or direct the mentee to relevant passages for further study.

- **Jesus' example:** The life of Jesus Christ exemplifies effective spiritual mentorship. He called His disciples to follow Him and learn from Him by living alongside Him. The disciples were invited to leave their previous occupations and walk in close fellowship with Jesus, observing His actions and learning from His teachings.

- **Investing time and living as examples:** Spiritual mentors invest time and effort in the lives of their mentees. This could involve living together temporarily or purposefully spending significant time together. By living out their faith in daily life, mentors provide practical examples of what it means to follow Christ.

- **Leading by example:** A mentor sets an example for their mentees to follow. St. Paul, the apostle, urged his followers to imitate him as he imitated Christ. This isn't an act of arrogance but a recognition of the mentor's responsibility to be a godly role model. While mentors are not without flaws, they strive to demonstrate godly qualities and principles.

- **Encouraging growth and imitation:** Mentorship involves encouraging growth and development in the mentees. Paul's instruction to Timothy to "study to show thyself approved" (*New International Version*, 2011/1973, 2 Timothy 2:15) emphasizes the importance of personal growth and a commitment to understanding the Word of God.

- **Creating a family atmosphere:** In some instances, spiritual mentorship involves close relationships akin to family. Young believers may temporarily live with more mature Christians to observe their lifestyle and learn from their example.

Spiritual mentorship is a vital aspect of all Abrahamic faiths, rooted in the sacred text's teachings. While the term "mentor" may not be explicitly used, the principles of teaching, leading by example, investing time, and encouraging growth are evident throughout Abrahamic Scriptures. The relationship between Jesus and His disciples serves as a foundational model for how believers can mentor and be mentored in their faith journey.

## Trusting Intuition and Inner Wisdom

Using your intuition to make decisions and navigate life's problems may be a great tool. Often, our gut feelings and inner instincts can guide us in the right direction, even when logic and analysis fall short. Here are some insights and strategies to help you develop and trust your intuition (Lillibridge, 2023):

- **Acknowledge the feeling:** Many people dismiss their intuitive feelings, rationalizing them as unfounded or irrational. Instead, recognize that intuition is a valid form of knowing and understanding. When you feel that something is off or right, acknowledge and validate that feeling.

- **Prioritize safety:** Your intuition is an internal warning system that can alert you to potential dangers or uncomfortable situations. It is critical to trust your instincts, especially when it comes to personal safety. Prioritize your well-being over societal expectations of politeness.

- **Understand intuition:** Intuition is a combination of your subconscious mind processing information and your accumulated life experiences. It's your brain making connections beyond conscious awareness. Recognize that intuition is not random; it's a result of your brain's remarkable pattern recognition abilities.

- **Practice self-awareness:** Tune into your body and emotions. Pay attention to how you feel in various situations. Notice any physical sensations, such as unease, tension, or a "gut feeling." Self-awareness enhances your ability to pick up on subtle signals from your intuition.

- **Reflect on past experiences:** Think back to instances when you trusted your intuition and it proved accurate. Remember the positive outcomes that resulted from listening to your inner wisdom. These reflections can build confidence in your intuitive abilities.

- **Create mental space:** Give yourself the time and mental space to make decisions. Avoid rushing into choices, especially if they are significant. Take a step back, breathe, and allow your intuition to guide you over time.

- **Embrace your better self:** Connect with the side of yourself that seeks growth, authenticity, and well-being. Engage in practices that align with your better self, such as mindfulness, meditation, or reading inspirational material.

- **Release negative energy:** Find healthy outlets to release negative emotions or stress. Physical activities like push-ups, running, or yoga can help release tension and allow your intuition to surface.

- **Seek trusted input:** While intuition is personal, seeking advice from people you trust can provide additional perspectives. Share your thoughts with those who listen without imposing their own agendas.

- **Practice decision-making:** Begin with small decisions to practice trusting your intuition. Gradually move on to more significant choices. Observe the outcomes and learn from each experience.

- **Stay true to yourself:** Stand up for what you believe is right, even if it contradicts others' expectations. Prepare responses to set boundaries politely and confidently when others question your choices.

- **Tune into physical signals:** Pay attention to how your body responds to different situations or people. Physical sensations, such as a knot in your stomach or raised hairs on your arms, can be intuitive cues.

- **Develop resilience:** Understand that not all intuitive decisions will lead to immediate positive outcomes. Sometimes, intuition guides you to important lessons or growth opportunities.

- **Cultivate patience:** Trusting your intuition is a journey that requires patience. Over time, as you practice and validate your intuitive insights, your trust will naturally strengthen.

Remember that trusting your intuition is about developing a deeper connection with yourself and honoring your inner wisdom. It's a skill that takes time and practice but can lead to more authentic and fulfilling life choices.

# Chapter 13:

# Rituals and Symbolism as Expressions of Faith

When it comes to religious observance, the significance of rituals and symbolism is unmistakable. These facets of faith carry deep spiritual meanings and serve as direct conduits to the divine.

Across the three Abrahamic belief systems, from ancient traditions to modern practices, rituals, and symbolism hold a pivotal role in fostering connections with the Creator.

This chapter delves into the essence of why rituals and symbolism matter—they serve as tangible expressions of the intangible—bringing believers closer to the core of their faith and enabling a profound communion with the divine.

## Symbolism in Sacred Objects

Concerning religious practices, the significance of sacred objects varies among the Abrahamic faiths. While Islam may not emphasize sacred items as intensely as Judaism and Christianity, there are items Muslims hold dear, particularly the Quran.

With its inception amidst a pagan culture, Islam sought to distance itself from idolatry and talismans. Devotion to anything other than Allah is viewed as a serious transgression.

Christianity, encompassing two billion adherents, showcases the cross as a widespread emblem. The Bible remains a universally revered artifact for Christians. Additional objects like the rosary and holy water carry religious weight for some.

Even though relics like the Shroud of Turin and fragments of the True Cross lack scientific verification, they possess mythic significance for many believers (Wynne, 2020).

Jewish practice features ritual objects, collectively known as Judaica, reflecting the principle of *hiddur mitzvah* or beautification of the commandment. Five primary symbols mark the Jewish faith (Shmelova, 2023):

1. In Jewish heritage, *challos*, playing a vital role in the Shabbat meal, symbolize unity and invoke blessings.

2. The Menorah, a seven-branched candelabrum, guards the Jewish community as an emblem of divine illumination.

3. During prayers, the Torah, serving as a spiritual compass, embodies the essence of Judaism.

4. Tombstones, known as *matzevot*, convey information about the deceased through their inscriptions.

5. The Star of David, a widely recognized hexagram, represents both protection and harmony, bearing the significance of King David's protective shield.

Though each faith uniquely reveres sacred objects, these symbols and artifacts collectively contribute to the rich tapestry of spirituality woven by the Abrahamic traditions.

# Rituals of Initiation and Rites of Passage

In Judaism, significant religious rituals mark various life events, underscoring the importance of tradition and faith. The birth of a child, whether a son or daughter, is celebrated joyously. The birth of a son involves the ritual of circumcision, symbolizing the commitment of the Jewish people to God's covenant.

Male circumcision is performed on the eighth day after birth, signifying the community's welcome to the newborn. This practice also holds significance even in challenging circumstances, as seen in the Former Soviet Union, where Jews organized circumcisions despite religious suppression (*Rites of passage*, n.d.).

The birth of a daughter is marked by the father being called to the Torah reading in the synagogue to pronounce a blessing and announce the baby's name. Over time, additional rituals like *Simchat Bat* or *Brit B'not Yisrael* have emerged to celebrate the birth of a daughter. These rituals often take place in the home and contribute to the sense of community and religious connection (*Rites of passage*, n.d.).

Another crucial life event is the Bar Mitzvah for boys and the Bat Mitzvah for girls. When a Jewish boy turns 13, he becomes responsible for observing the commandments of the Torah. The Bar Mitzvah ceremony includes reading from the Torah, symbolizing this transition.

Similarly, the Bat Mitzvah for girls, often held around the age of 12, has become an integral part of Jewish practice. In some congregations, it mirrors the Bar Mitzvah ceremony, while others have developed distinct rituals and readings for girls.

These ceremonies emphasize religious obligations and strengthen the connection to Jewish identity and community.

They create opportunities for family and friends to gather and celebrate, fostering a sense of belonging and continuity with Jewish tradition.

Religious rituals and ceremonies are significant in various aspects of religious life. In Christianity, the sacraments are central to worship and the expression of faith. Baptism, a rite of initiation, symbolizes spiritual cleansing and rebirth in Christ.

The Eucharist, also known as Holy Communion, commemorates the Last Supper and represents the unity of believers through the sharing of bread and wine. Other sacraments include confirmation, reconciliation (confession), ordination of ministers, and anointing of the sick (*Rites and ceremonies,* n.d.).

Similarly, religious practices hold great importance in Islam and guide various life events. Male circumcision is a religious obligation based on a divine command and is performed to signify a commitment to God. Marriage is a joyous occasion that involves reading Quranic passages, followed by a feast, uniting two individuals before God and their community (*Rites and ceremonies,* n.d.).

The rituals surrounding death emphasize the significance of the afterlife, with the deceased being buried promptly and prayers being recited to aid the soul's journey to the next life.

Abrahamic religions emphasize the role of rituals in connecting believers with their faith and community, marking important life transitions, and expressing devotion to their respective deities. These practices serve as tangible expressions of religious beliefs and values, reinforcing the sense of belonging and purpose within their religious communities.

# Healing Rituals and Blessing

Like many other faiths, Judaism offers many spiritual practices to navigate illness, suffering, and loss. Rooted in tradition and community, Judaism has cultivated various practices that provide meaning, guidance, comfort, and solace during these challenging times. Among these practices is the deeply meaningful act of adding a Jewish name for someone dealing with a serious illness.

The practice of adding a Jewish name holds immense spiritual significance. Names in Judaism are not merely labels; they carry deep meanings and connections to one's identity and heritage. The community affirms their solidarity, recognition, and support by adding a Jewish name for someone facing illness. This act is a testament to the interconnectedness of individuals within the community and the belief in the power of collective prayers (Beliefnet, 2016).

Furthermore, the prayer ritual is central to Judaism's healing approach. While prayer is encouraged, its essence lies beyond mere repetition of words. The teachings of figures like Jesus emphasize that prayer should come with sincerity and intention from the heart. Prayer becomes a channel to connect with the divine; the practice can provide inner solace and strength.

Meditation practices also find their place in Christianity. Jesus' advice to pray in private and connect with the Divine Essence within resonates with the concept of meditation. This internal practice, conducted away from external distractions, allows individuals to connect with the sacred space within themselves and align their consciousness with the Divine presence.

In Islamic traditions, water plays a pivotal role in healing and spirituality. The Quran's reference to water as the source of all creation underscores its importance. Healing bowls, often inscribed with sacred words and verses, exemplify the connection between water, written prayers, and healing (*The arts of protection and healing in Islam*, 2021).

These bowls, used for tending to the sick and divining the future, hold therapeutic potential due to the sacredness of the inscribed words. Similarly, metal tags inscribed with invocations function like prayer beads, connecting the spoken word with material objects.

The practice of healing bowls was also associated with female fertility and childbirth. Using such bowls for fertility rituals and protection against evil spirits highlights Islamic traditions' intricate relationship between faith, symbolism, and healing.

In the Abrahamic faiths, the intertwining of spirituality, healing, and rituals showcases the deep-rooted belief that faith can provide solace and strength during times of illness and adversity. These practices offer guidance and support and emphasize the interconnectedness of individuals within their respective communities.

## Marriage and Wedding Rituals

Religious wedding traditions within the context of Judaism, Christianity, and Islam—reflect each religion's deep-rooted spiritual values and principles. While there are distinct differences, there are also some common threads that run through their marriage customs. Here, we delve into these traditions' origins, similarities, and differences.

One significant similarity across Judaism, Christianity, and Islam is the emphasis on marrying within the same faith. In all three traditions, the religious laws discourage interfaith marriages.

This principle is rooted in the belief that shared faith forms a strong foundation for a harmonious marital relationship and the upbringing of children within a unified religious framework.

## *Jewish Marriage Traditions*

- **Arranged marriages:** Historically, arranged marriages were common in Jewish communities. Using a *shadchan* (matchmaker) to facilitate marriages is a practice that aims to ensure compatibility based on shared values and beliefs.

- **Engagement and ketubah:** Jewish engagement, known as *erusin*, involves the couple's commitment to marry by exchanging documents. The *ketubah*, a marriage contract, outlines the husband's obligations to his wife.

- **Bedeken ceremony:** Just before the wedding ceremony, the groom veils the bride in a tradition known as the *bedeken*. This gesture recalls the story of Jacob and ensures the groom is marrying the intended bride.

- **Sheva brachot:** During the wedding ceremony, seven blessings called *sheva brachot* are recited, celebrating the union and invoking blessings for the couple's future.

## Christian Marriage Traditions

- **Unity in faith:** Christian marriage is rooted in the New Testament teaching that believers should marry fellow believers (*New International Version,* 2011/1973, 2 Corinthians 6:14).

- **Sacramental significance:** Marriage is considered a sacrament in many Christian denominations, signifying a sacred covenant before God and the community.

- **Wedding ceremony:** The wedding ceremony often includes vows, the exchange of rings, and a sermon or message on the spiritual significance of marriage.

## Islamic Marriage Traditions

- **Arranged marriages:** Similar to Jewish tradition, arranged marriages are common in Islamic culture, with families playing a role in finding suitable partners based on shared faith and values.

- **Engagement and marriage contract:** Islamic marriage involves an engagement phase during which a marriage contract, known as a *Nikah*, is agreed upon. This contract outlines the rights and responsibilities of both partners.

- **Henna ceremony:** The henna ceremony is a pre-wedding ritual involving the application of henna dye to the bride's hands and feet. It is a joyful event filled with music and celebration.

- **Marriage ceremony:** The Islamic marriage ceremony, *Nikah*, involves reciting vows and the signing of the marriage contract. The couple's union is celebrated with prayers and community participation.

## Differences in Perspective

Despite these similarities, there are differences in perspective. For example, in Christianity, marriage is generally celebrated as a joyful and positive institution, while in Islam and Judaism, there's an emphasis on the practical and spiritual aspects of marriage, including maintaining a family and adhering to religious laws.

- **Symbolism and meaning:** The symbolism of marriage varies across these traditions. In Christianity, marriage is often viewed as a reflection of Christ's relationship with the Church, emphasizing sacrificial love and unity. Marriage is the foundation for building a Jewish home and community in Judaism. In Islam, marriage is considered a source of mutual support and protection.

- **Joy and sorrow:** Across these faiths, wedding ceremonies are marked by both joy and solemnity. While there is celebration, there's also an acknowledgment of the commitment's weight and the potential challenges ahead.

- **Future considerations:** In today's interconnected world, interfaith marriages are more common. While the Abrahamic traditions discourage interfaith unions due to potential challenges in maintaining religious unity and raising children, the approach to interfaith marriages varies among individuals, religious leaders, and communities.

The marriage traditions within Judaism, Christianity, and Islam are shaped by their religious teachings, historical practices, and cultural contexts. While they each have unique features, the common thread of marrying within the same faith reflects the central role of religion in shaping marital relationships and family life.

## Funeral and Mourning Rituals

Funeral customs are deeply rooted in culture and reflect attitudes and beliefs surrounding death. The funeral traditions in the Abrahamic religions, including Islam, Judaism, Christianity, and Eastern Orthodox Christianity, vary but also share similarities.

Islam, Judaism, and Christianity all advocate for burial as the appropriate way to handle the deceased. The origin of this practice is traced back to the story of Cain and Abel. Both Muslims and Jews follow this burial custom based on their respective holy texts. Islam and Judaism strictly prohibit cremation and embalming, and they prioritize prompt burials as a mark of respect for the deceased.

In Islam and Judaism, the body is washed and dressed in white burial shrouds. Muslims perform *ghusl*, while Jews perform the *Tahara*. A communal funeral prayer occurs at a mosque for Muslims and at a synagogue for Jews. The body is then laid to rest in a simple casket, and the deceased is positioned facing a specific direction (Mecca for Muslims and the qibla for Jews).

Christian funeral practices differ between Catholicism and Eastern Orthodox Christianity. Catholicism allows embalming and permits cremation but prefers it after the funeral. The Requiem Mass is an essential Catholic ritual. Eastern Orthodox practices involve a procession, Divine Liturgy, and prayers for the deceased.

Throughout these traditions, mourners express their grief and seek comfort by connecting with their faith. Although specific practices vary, the core principles of showing reverence for the departed and supporting the grieving are universal.

## Pilgrimage and Sacred Journey Rituals

Pilgrimage serves as a symbolic representation of the human journey on Earth, embodying a search for truth and spiritual exploration. Individuals from various regions gather at a central point, drawn by a spiritual force.

This practice signifies the pursuit of a connection with the Ultimate Reality and the aspiration to attain harmony within oneself and with the surroundings. Virtually all major religious traditions underscore the significance of pilgrimage, assigning it a central role in their faith (*Pilgrimage in different religions,* 2022).

Human existence, according to Christianity, is seen as a pilgrimage from an ultimate home to a past paradise. The promise of restoration is believed to redeem the fall from grace through the coming of the Son of God. Christian pilgrimage's essence is grounded in the remembrance of Jesus.

Life, as a pilgrimage toward eternal peace, is considered by believers to stand between Edenic memories and a yearning for heavenly return. Therefore, the specific pilgrimage destination holds less significance than the overall spiritual journey. Sites associated with Jesus' life were actively sought out by devotees, fostering a spiritual connection with his experiences. Jerusalem, linked to Jesus' earthly life, became a focal point of pilgrimage.

In Islam, a fundamental duty for Muslims who have the means is the Hajj pilgrimage. The act of pilgrimage to Mecca finds its roots in the trials of Abraham and his family. The Hajj, obligatory for capable Muslims, is the fifth pillar of Islam. Unlike other religious pilgrimages, it is mandatory.

The rituals of Hajj, including circumambulating the Kaaba, walking between Safa and Marwah, standing at Mount Arafat, throwing stones at pillars, and performing a sacrificial offering, trace back to Abraham's actions. These rituals serve as a means to achieve Allah's forgiveness. Under the common banner of faith, Hajj unites diverse pilgrims, transcending cultural and ethnic boundaries (*Pilgrimage in different religions*, 2022).

The roots of pilgrimage in Judaism can be traced back to the narrative of Adam and Eve. Their once harmonious relationship with God was disrupted, leading to human efforts to seek reconciliation. The concept of exile is deeply embedded in Jewish history, originating from God's selection of Abraham as the progenitor of a chosen people.

The journey of the Jews from Egypt to Palestine is characterized by periods of both wandering and settling. Jerusalem occupies a central position in this narrative, closely associated with the Ark of the Covenant, which symbolizes God's presence. Jewish tradition mandates three annual festivals—Pesach (Passover), Shavuot (Feast of Weeks), and Sukkot (Feast of Booths)—that necessitate a pilgrimage to Jerusalem. These festivals commemorate pivotal moments in Jewish history and are observed with great reverence.

Pilgrimage is a powerful representation of the spiritual journey and quest for truth in Abrahamic religions. Whether in Judaism, Christianity, or Islam, the act of pilgrimage reflects the human longing to connect with the Divine and lead a harmonious existence.

# Rituals of Repentance and Forgiveness

Reconciliation, often referred to as "Confession," is a sacramental ritual that serves as a celebration through which individuals who have committed serious transgressions against God or fellow human beings, known as "Mortal" or deadly sins, seek forgiveness and restoration. This process aims to reconcile them both with God and the Christian community, represented by the Church (Fisch, n.d.).

The core components of this ritual involve the sinner openly confessing their sins to a priest or bishop, who represents the entire Church. Following the confession, the priest or bishop offers a prayer of absolution, signifying forgiveness, and the individual undertakes a form of restitution, referred to as "penance," as an act of atonement for their actions (Fisch, n.d.).

The person's relationship with God and the Church is restored through this process. The prayer spoken by the priest or bishop during this ritual signifies the declaration of God's forgiveness of the individual's sins.

A central challenge in cultural and religious efforts to promote peace is the tendency to create boundaries around ethnic and religious identities. These boundaries can restrict the development of positive moral values and systems of meaning. Within the Abrahamic traditions, ethical tools can contribute to peacemaking and resolving conflicts. One crucial aspect is how individuals and communities deal with moral shortcomings.

In the context of intercultural interactions, understanding how these traditions handle moral failures is essential. Often, an outsider group becomes the target of strained relationships. However, these relationships might be transformed through traditional processes that involve acknowledging wrongdoing and seeking forgiveness. The concept of sin and the act of seeking forgiveness play significant roles in this transformation.

The intricate facets and applications of forgiveness and reconciliation within Christianity, Judaism, and Islam are thoroughly examined. The analysis suggests that all three of these religions hold the potential to utilize reconciliation as a means of conflict resolution. Ultimately, these traditions offer pathways for repairing relationships and promoting peace.

In Judaism, the concepts of repentance and forgiveness are regarded as fundamental to the human experience, and Judaism offers a framework for their realization. These principles hold great significance because, without them, individuals can remain disconnected from one another and from God, potentially leading to a cycle of vengeance, violence, and separation from the divine (Fisch, n.d.).

However, the process of forgiveness is not simple to attain and is not universally applicable in all circumstances. Genuine repentance, sincere remorse, and appropriate restitution are prerequisites for earning forgiveness.

For forgiveness to be granted, the act of repentance must address the wrongs committed in the past, work to mend the wounds inflicted on both the physical and spiritual levels, and demonstrate a genuine commitment to refraining from repeating the transgression in the future.

Nevertheless, there may be instances where forgiveness cannot be fully achieved, especially in cases of grave offenses. In particular, the perpetrators of the Holocaust, who inflicted unimaginable suffering, may face challenges in attaining forgiveness, especially if they did not or could not engage in a genuine act of repentance (Dobkowski, n.d.).

The question of whether forgiveness can be extended to them remains uncertain and open-ended. Only the Most High God is the Supreme Judge, and only He knows what is best.

# Chapter 14:

# Unity in Diversity—Embracing Differences

In a world often fragmented by misunderstanding and mistrust, acknowledging our shared humanity becomes a bridge that spans the divides.

Beneath the surface differences in rituals, symbols, and doctrines lies a common thread that unites us in our hopes, dreams, and aspirations.

Regardless of our religious affiliations, cultural backgrounds, or geographic origins, we are united by the fundamental experiences of joy, sorrow, love, and longing.

Just as a garden flourishes with a variety of flowers, our world flourishes when we nurture and cultivate the diverse beliefs that shape the thoughts and actions of people across cultures.

May we strive to understand, appreciate, and learn from one another's faiths, recognizing that in this grand design, every portion is essential to the beauty of the whole.

# Embracing Religious Diversity

Diverse faith communities across the expanse of the European continent are facing deteriorating conditions. A reevaluation of the approach and the cessation of granting Europe a "free pass" concerning human rights, particularly religious freedom, are deemed necessary by advocates.

Countries widely acknowledged for religious freedom violations often receive prioritized attention from human rights advocates, inadvertently causing them to overlook nations like France, Germany, Belgium, Montenegro, Bulgaria, and the Netherlands, where similar issues exist. However, this oversight is considered a critical mistake (Moore & Turkel, 2020).

Consider the concerning trend among European Jews. Recent data reveals that nearly four out of ten European Jews contemplate leaving their home countries due to safety fears stemming from experiencing anti-Semitic incidents. Alarming spikes in anti-Semitism aren't limited to certain countries but rather stretch across Europe, with notable increases in France, Germany, and the Netherlands (Moore & Turkel, 2020).

Yet, these numbers don't fully capture the gravity of the situation. Physical attacks on Jewish people and institutions are occurring in multiple European nations, painting a stark picture of the dangers these communities face.

Adding to the complexity, certain religious practices are now under legal scrutiny. For instance, Belgium is considering a ban on *shechita*, the traditional Jewish method of animal slaughter (Moore & Turkel, 2020). Similarly, Muslim practices are also targeted. These actions have raised concerns and sparked criticism from various quarters.

This issue transcends anti-Semitism alone; religious freedom conditions throughout Europe are in decline. Government restrictions on religious activities have surged from 2007 to 2017, a trend linked to an increase in violent attacks and discrimination against Muslims. Instances like France's ban on full facial coverings in 2011 and the prohibition of public Muslim worship in Moldova in 2012 illustrate the growing restrictions (Moore & Turkel, 2020).

The broader ramifications of diminishing religious liberties are evident, stretching beyond specific religious communities. For instance, Montenegro is currently witnessing ongoing protests due to apprehensions about government encroachment on religious properties as a result of a recent religious law.

Europe's commitment to worldwide religious freedom appears to be waning, as illustrated by the choice not to extend the mandate of the European Union's (EU) Special Envoy for Freedom of Religion and Belief. This underscores a disconcerting facet of Europe's approach.

Another troubling facet pertains to Europe's position on China, especially in light of China's policies that target Jews, Muslims, and Christians. Some European leaders seem to downplay these concerns, despite the United Nations' forceful condemnations. This inconsistency raises doubts about Europe's true dedication to religious freedom.

Europe should draw lessons from its history as a stark reminder of the hazards of religious persecution and its potential fallout, which includes the eradication of cultures, ethnic cleansing, and even genocide. This historical consciousness should inspire Europe to maintain the same standards it advocates for on a global scale.

# Tolerance and Respect

This section illuminates the foundations laid when Prophet Muhammad himself engaged with people of differing faiths, illustrating practical instances from his life. The high level of tolerance exhibited by the prophet toward individuals of various beliefs is best encapsulated by the Quranic verse: "To your religion be yours, and to my religion be mine" (*The Holy Quran*, 2016, 109:06). In the era of the prophet, the Arabian Peninsula housed a multitude of faiths, encompassing Christians, Jews, Zoroastrians, polytheists, and those without religious affiliations. A careful examination of his life discloses numerous instances revealing his profound tolerance toward individuals of diverse faiths (Abdulsalam, 2006).

To comprehend the breadth of this tolerance, it's vital to consider the period when Islam emerged as an established state, governed by the prophet according to religious principles. While instances of tolerance by the prophet during his thirteen years in Mecca exist, some may attribute them to the elevation of the status of Muslims and Islam. Hence, the focus shifts to the period commencing with his migration to Medina and the formulation of the constitution.

The constitution, also recognized as the *Saheefah*, serves as an embodiment of the prophet's tolerance toward other religions. Upon relocating to Medina, the prophet transitioned from a religious leader to a political one. The constitution was meticulously designed to foster harmony and stability in a society that accommodated Muslims, Jews, Christians, and polytheists. It delineates the duties, responsibilities, and constraints applicable to all residents of Medina. Compliance with its provisions was expected from everyone with any breach regarded as an act of betrayal.

One of the fundamental principles enshrined in the constitution was the unity of all inhabitants of Medina, irrespective of their faith. All groups were regarded as constituents of a unified nation, and this inclusiveness extended to safeguarding individuals from different religious backgrounds. The prophet's interactions guaranteed the security and impartial treatment of individuals with diverse faiths. For instance, he vehemently cautioned against harming those who had entered into truces with the Muslims, emphasizing that such actions would result in the forfeiture of Paradise.

Furthermore, the prophet underscored the significance of treating individuals from other faiths with respect and honor. He issued stern warnings against mistreating minorities who did not follow Islam, proclaiming that he would personally intercede on their behalf on the Day of Judgment.

The constitution also expressly recognized the distinct religions of its inhabitants. Each religious community was granted the freedom to practice its beliefs without external interference. Moreover, any conflicts or disputes were to be referred to God and His Messenger for resolution, underscoring a superior authority that transcended individual leaders. This provision acknowledged the autonomy of each religion in its internal matters, provided they did not contravene the principles outlined in the Constitution.

Prophet Muhammad's interactions with individuals of other faiths unequivocally manifest a profound level of religious tolerance. The Constitution instituted in Medina, which placed emphasis on unity, safeguarding minority rights, and showing reverence for divergent beliefs, stands as a testament to his unwavering commitment to promoting coexistence and harmony among diverse communities (Abdulsalam, 2006).

# Celebrating Cultural Expressions

Jesus at an earlier time in his ministry iterated: "Blessed are the peacemakers, for they will be called children of God" (Studzinski, 2017).

As we entered the middle of April 2022, it became increasingly clear that the world was facing a series of unprecedented challenges. Emerging from a pandemic, we found ourselves grappling with global, environmental, and economic crises. It became evident that relying solely on governments for solutions was inadequate (Studzinski, 2022).

Remarkably, unity did not require homogeneity. Despite the distinctive customs and meanings associated with Ramadan, Passover, and Easter, these observances shared common threads of self-denial, fostering goodwill, and promoting peace. Muslims commemorated the Quran's revelation, Jews relived the liberation from enslavement, and Christians celebrated the Resurrection. All these practices aimed to strengthen the connection with the divine.

Interestingly, this prevailing gloom coincided with a unique alignment of the lunar calendar that carried significant meaning for all three Abrahamic religions. April 2022 saw the observance of annual festivals crucial to Muslims, Jews, Catholics, and Protestants. Ramadan, commencing on April 1st and lasting a month, was in progress; Passover began on the evening of April 15th, followed by Easter Sunday on April 17th for Catholics and Protestants, with Orthodox Easter a week later.

These leaders, with their courage, passion, and insight, inspired others to join them in pursuing compassion, justice, and freedom while preserving the world. They were willing to make sacrifices and confront challenges, understanding that letting differences become insurmountable barriers was counterproductive.

As Mother Theresa often said, "Change the world one person at a time." While these faiths shared monotheism, they were not monolithic. It was up to individuals to harness their potential, exercising integrity and dignity in personal and professional spheres. This could manifest as acts of faith, freedom of speech, ethical business conduct, support for refugees, or advocacy for peace, among others (Studzinski, 2017).

The pandemic had underscored the importance of collective efforts for a just cause. The response to the Ukrainian conflict highlighted the value of collaboration for shared objectives and the greater good. This reiterated the idea that what unites humanity is greater than what divides it. Embracing our individual identities, whether religious or not, and recognizing the distinctive contributions of others allowed us to find purpose within the broader framework.

Jesus, at an earlier time in his ministry, iterated: "Blessed are the peacemakers, for they will be called children of God" (*New International Version,* 2011/1973, Matthew 5:9; Studzinski, 2017).

## Overcoming Religious Prejudice

Titled *How We Coexist*, a research report conducted by the Woolf Institute spanning two years highlights the significant role of religion as a frontier for personal bias. It contends that negative perceptions associated with religious attitudes outweigh those influenced by ethnicity or nationality (Sherwood, 2020).

Based on a survey of 11,700 individuals in England and Wales, the study concludes that, while many individuals exhibit tolerance toward those from diverse ethnic or national backgrounds, a substantial proportion harbors unfavorable attitudes linked to religion. The research underscores the critical role of religion, especially concerning Muslims (Sherwood, 2020).

Survey findings indicate that nearly three-quarters of non-Black or Asian respondents feel comfortable with the idea of a close relative marrying a black or Asian individual. However, only 43% share the same level of comfort when it comes to a close relative marrying a Muslim (Sherwood, 2020).

Furthermore, the research reveals that Muslims often confront negative attitudes from individuals belonging to other religious groups. Intriguingly, many Muslims themselves also tend to maintain unfavorable attitudes toward individuals of different faiths (Sherwood, 2020).

To evaluate tolerance and bias, the researchers focused their investigation on attitudes related to intermarriage. In general, the public holds positive views about intermarriage across ethnic and national boundaries. However, the term "Muslim" elicits more negative sentiment compared to the term "Pakistani," despite a significant proportion of British Pakistanis being Muslim (Sherwood, 2020).

The prevalence of religious-based prejudice is more pronounced among individuals aged over 75, those with limited educational qualifications, people from non-Asian ethnic minorities, and Baptist Christians. Interestingly, men tend to exhibit more discomfort than women when contemplating the prospect of a close relative marrying someone from a diverse ethnic, national, or religious background (Sherwood, 2020).

In various religious communities, including Hindus, Sikhs, Jews, Buddhists, and individuals with no religious affiliation, a majority expressed unease about the possibility of a close relative marrying a Muslim. Within the Christian community, a notable minority shares this sentiment (Sherwood, 2020).

## Interreligious Peacebuilding

Today, the various Abrahamic faith traditions across the globe hold a pivotal role in fostering harmonious peace accompanied by justice, both within local communities and on a global scale. The relationships that unfold between different religions function as bridges, connecting people in our ever-more interconnected world.

These interactions, which encompass the exploration of disparities as well as shared values, stand as essential components as we strive to comprehend one another and identify collaborative approaches to extend support.

The emphasis on peace draws us deeper into our ongoing endeavors and commitments in the realm of interreligious relations, whether as individuals or as a collective council. It compels us to transcend beyond mere dialogues and acts of solidarity, both of which remain crucial in the scope of interreligious relations and must persist.

It urges us to transition into active participants in peacebuilding alongside neighbors of varying faiths, serving our collective existence as religious communities, our society, and our world at large. This shift fosters collaboration, allowing us to develop a more profound understanding of one another as Jews, Christians, and Muslims and as fellow inhabitants within our religiously diverse milieu.

In doing so, we can jointly establish a shared agenda with our spiritual brothers and sisters for the pursuit of peace through interreligious engagement. We are called to adopt a stance of humility, where we both extend and accept hospitality. It is through this posture that we collectively shape a vision of equitable peace in tandem with our neighbors of diverse faiths—outside of the Abrahamic family tree.

In the broader cultural context, in the United States, we bear witness to an escalating division and polarization. Acts of racism, white nationalism, anti-immigrant sentiments, and xenophobia.

In the United States, within the broader cultural context, we observe an escalating division and polarization. Instances of racism, white nationalism, anti-immigrant sentiments, and xenophobia have become increasingly evident.

In regions spanning Europe, Asia, and Africa, a troubling increase in incidents of religious bigotry, often invoking the names of our respective faiths, is cause for alarm. This situation emphasizes the pressing need for us to wholeheartedly adopt interreligious engagement as a vehicle for nurturing peace on local, national, and global scales.

It's been more than 400 years since the forced displacement and enslavement of African people; it is of paramount importance to recognize the historical role played by Abrahamic religions in restricting the religious freedom of indigenous and enslaved communities.

The enduring and deeply ingrained legacy of racism, exemplified by the ongoing crisis of mass incarceration disproportionately affecting black individuals, remains a deeply troubling concern. As adherents of Judaism, Christianity, and Islam, we bear the responsibility to address these issues head-on and affirm that our faith unequivocally condemns harmful rhetoric and violent acts, considering them entirely incompatible with the teachings of God.

In this dynamic and ever-evolving context, the Abrahamic faiths acknowledge the growing importance of interreligious engagement. This acknowledgment is evident through the continuation of longstanding dialogues between Jewish and Muslim-Christian counterparts. Furthermore, there is a need to strengthen and expand these dialogues to include new interactions with Buddhists, Hindus, and Sikhs.

Our motivations for engaging in interreligious dialogue are deeply rooted in pastoral, theological, and communal considerations. Within the Abrahamic faiths, we are called to practice love for our neighbors, a mission that requires us to become familiar with those who share our communities and the wider world.

During this process of engaging in dialogues, we emphasize the inherent worth of every human being, recognizing them as our fellow siblings. We frequently uncover both shared values and differences in how we perceive ourselves, our understanding of the divine, and our commitment to social justice and peace.

Our own faith can be nurtured, and creative pathways for manifesting that faith can be explored through our engagement. While the responsibility of conveying the message of the One God of Creation is affirmed by Abrahamic believers, the inclusion of proselytism as an inappropriate element in interreligious engagement is firmly rejected.

The most genuine expression of our love for the God of Abraham is reflected in our commitment to evangelism when our love and service are directed toward our neighbors as integral members of a united community.

Our belief in the concept of the Almighty God of the Universe is most accurately mirrored by this form of love.

# Chapter 15:

# Cultivating Soulful Connections

Within the spirituality of Jewish life, prayer and observance serve as conduits for a soulful connection with the Creator.

Christianity, marked by the teachings of Christ, directs our gaze inward and outward simultaneously.

Within Islam, the Five Pillars stand as pillars of connection, binding individuals to their faith and to one another.

The regularity of prayer, the commitment to charity, and the pilgrimage to Mecca serve as compass points in the journey of connection.

Self-reflection involves the art of introspection, offering us a clear mirror to examine our thoughts, emotions, and actions with impartiality.

Through this process, adherents of all three Abrahamic faiths foster an understanding of their own being, unraveling the layers of their consciousness in a profound and curious manner.

Inner Reflection and Self-Awareness

As we delve into this section on self-reflection, we embark on a journey of self-discovery that prompts us to question the origin of our feelings. The inquiry "Why do I feel this way?" becomes our guide, propelling us to explore the depths of our inner landscape.

The significance of self-reflection cannot be underestimated, yet it warrants caution against slipping into an obsessive mindset. Instead of becoming ensnared in its grip, the true essence of self-reflection lies in its capacity to drive us toward growth, positivity, and a sense of contentment.

At its core, self-reflection is a cultivated skill, a form of heightened self-awareness that touches upon various dimensions (Habash, 2022):

- **The physical:** Our bodily sensations and experiences.

- **The mental:** The landscape of our thoughts and cognitions.

- **The emotional:** The intricate tapestry of our feelings and sentiments.

- **The spiritual:** Our connection to a more profound sense of self and the universe.

In engaging with self-reflection, we forge an inner witness within ourselves, an observer that peers into our being from a gentle distance. This lens allows us to scrutinize not just the surface but also the layers beneath—much like gazing into a mirror that reflects our appearance and essence.

This practice propels us to embrace our thoughts, behaviors, and emotions with inquisitiveness. It encourages us to move beyond the surface and embark on a quest for understanding (Habash, 2022):

- What are the origins of these thoughts?

- What truly lies behind this veil of sadness?

- Could there be a deeper layer beneath this anxiety?

- What is the body communicating through these sensations?

With regard to personal growth, self-reflection is an indispensable tool. It rescues us from unconscious reactivity, empowering us to choose healthier responses and reshaping unproductive behaviors and thoughts. It's a compass that guides us toward conscious choices, preventing us from reacting impulsively or uttering words we may later regret (Habash, 2022).

While self-reflection promises infinite depths, moderation is key. Should self-reflection morph into self-critique, it loses its essence. A vigilant eye is needed to ensure that our introspection remains a neutral observer, not a breeding ground for self-judgment. It's a fine line between constructive reflection and corrosive comparison. Self-reflection should inspire us to embrace self-compassion, listen to our inner wisdom, and cultivate an atmosphere of positive change.

Through this practice, we transcend the ordinary and embark on a transformative journey toward deeper understanding, greater compassion, and a more profound connection with ourselves and the world around us.

# Nature as a Source of Inspiration

The intricate laws of nature are intricately etched into the very fabric of the Earth, concealed within its crevices and faults. Guiding us to comprehend these laws is a pathway to unveiling the wisdom of the author of all laws, a journey of enlightenment whose starting point is the natural kingdom.

Nature serves as a wellspring of inspiration for humanity. Echoing the sentiments of Albert Einstein, who remarked that our grasp of nature's revelations is minuscule, it is apparent that nature's teachings are profound. Amidst the hustle and bustle, where chaos, competition, and negativity prevail, nature emerges as a sanctuary of happiness, equality, encouragement, and tranquility. Within its embrace, we can sense the creation of a Higher Power—a testament to a divinity that transcends falsehood and hypocrisy (Singh, 2012).

Inspiration abounds, woven seamlessly into the tapestry of existence. From the radiance of dawn to the serenity of dusk, from the morning's first sip of tea to the evening's final meal, inspiration is omnipresent. It is a perpetual current that defies definition, influenced by the intricacies of our psyche and channeling positive responses to our experiences. A source of motivation can stem from the humble ant to the complex human experience, drawing from both nature's elements and its deviations from the norm.

Nature's splendor elicits a blend of awe and admiration that inspires us. This simple enchantment infuses our encounters with greater significance, resonating in the scenes, sounds, and scents that enliven our senses. From the grace of deer in a meadow to the melodic symphony of a meandering stream, these moments become the foundation upon which we construct our aspirations and kindle our fervor for the road ahead (Singh, 2012).

In the words of Ralph Waldo Emerson, "To go into solitude, a man needs to retire as much from his chamber as from society" (Singh, 2012). Indeed, solitude is the conduit through which we can grasp nature's offerings fully. In nature's embrace, the reciprocal relationship between humanity and its surroundings takes shape, unveiling a spiritual kinship. The wisdom of nature intertwines with our being, fostering mutual enrichment as the wind sows the seed, the sun nurtures growth, and the cycles of life continue in perpetual harmony.

Simplicity emerges as an enigmatic wonder among the dawn chorus of sparrows and the ephemeral dance of trees in the mist. Nature ignites the spark of ingenuity, beckoning humanity to unravel its puzzles. As the world evolves, the duality of nature's diversity and man's contemplation thereof emerges as a central theme, illuminating the intricate unity within the mystique of existence.

The interplay between man and nature necessitates a harmonious coexistence. Man can forge a profound connection with the natural world by forsaking societal distractions. Embracing solitude enables the symbiotic relationship between nature and man to flourish. The quest for answers to spiritual inquiries about matter, origin, and purpose drives us to recognize the intrinsic harmony that exists between nature and humanity. This fusion forms the essence of worship, where spiritual questions of what and where find solace (Singh, 2012).

In the end, nature responds in kind to our approach. A serene disposition opens the doors to a symphony of melodies and scents that soothe our mind, body, and spirit. Nature's creatures extend their curiosity in welcome, forging connections that transcend mere alarm. As we open ourselves to the teachings of nature, we experience a mutual influence that enriches our lives, echoing the timeless wisdom: "The tree which moves some to tears of joy is in the eyes of others only a green thing that stands in the way. Some see nature as all ridicule and deformity, and some scarcely see nature at all. But to the eyes of the man of imagination, nature is imagination itself" (Singh, 2012).

In this unending journey, we find ourselves drawn to the captivating synergy between the butterfly and the flower. Their communion is a testament to the harmony arising from a not-knowing state, a humility that aligns with nature's rhythm. Through such a lens, we learn to embrace the unknown and follow the course set by nature itself.

Together, nature and humanity navigate an ever-evolving relationship that embodies life's deepest wisdoms. As we bask in nature's embrace, our hearts resonate with its truths, revealing the intricate design that intertwines us with the essence of existence.

## Artistic Expression and Creativity

Evidence indicates that engaging in artistic endeavors can alleviate symptoms of depression and other mental health issues. Throughout history, artists have often been depicted as tormented souls who channel their pain into creative expression. But how accurate is this portrayal of the "tortured artist"?

Anecdotal evidence suggests a correlation between creative people and depression, with some asserting that depression can intensify creative output. However, scientific research provides a more nuanced perspective.

While specific studies have found connections between creativity and depression, no definitive evidence exists that one directly causes the other. Creative activities have been shown to positively impact mental health and mood disorders. Engaging in various art forms, such as painting, dancing, or writing, offers an outlet for processing emotions and alleviating symptoms of depression and other mental health conditions.

Numerous studies have explored the interplay between creativity and mental illness, particularly mood disorders. While research has associated creativity with specific conditions like bipolar disorder, the relationship between creativity and depression remains less concrete and requires further investigation (Telloian, 2021).

Can being creative help manage depression? Embracing creative activities with an open mind, regardless of whether one considers themselves an artist, can yield significant health benefits. Engaging in creativity provides a platform to explore and understand emotions, uplifts mood, and enhances self-esteem. Moreover, creative pursuits serve as a means of focusing the mind, like meditation, facilitating the processing of life experiences, and potentially alleviating depression symptoms.

The link between mood disorders and creativity prompts inquiries about whether artists are more prone to such conditions. Studies exploring this connection yield mixed results. Research has examined the similarities between hypomanic episodes and intense creativity, noting shared symptoms like deep concentration and an altered sense of time. However, no conclusive evidence supports a direct correlation (Telloian, 2021).

While certain studies suggest a higher susceptibility to mood disorders among creative individuals, diagnoses do not necessarily correlate with heightened creativity. Bipolar disorder has shown the closest association with creativity. Moreover, research analyzing over a million Swedish citizens found a link between creative careers and bipolar disorder diagnoses, possibly due to the high-stress nature of these professions (Telloian, 2021).

Creative activities enhance holistic well-being by boosting self-esteem, elevating mood, fostering a sense of accomplishment, improving memory, relieving stress, aiding self-discovery, and promoting focus and calmness. Writing, drawing, singing, and movement have all been found to improve mental health.

While the relationship between creativity and depression has been studied extensively, no concrete evidence suggests that depression inherently boosts creativity or that creative expression leads to depression. Instead, creative activities often mitigate depression symptoms, offering a sense of achievement, calmness, and joy.

For those struggling with depression, seeking support from healthcare or mental health professionals is crucial, as various treatments, including psychotherapy, cognitive behavioral therapy, support groups, medication, and art therapy, are available.

## Music and Sacred Sounds

Through the passage of time, sacred sounds have functioned as a profound conduit for various human cultures to explore profound inquiries, convey their beliefs, extol their devotions, and motivate others to follow a path into the enigmas of existence, both earthly and cosmic. This spectrum of sacred sound traditions encompasses a cornucopia of expressive forms encompassing melodious and repetitive vocalizations known as chants, fervent and emotionally charged hums, groans, and shouts, as well as rhythmic hand claps, foot stomps, and intricate song compositions.

These instrumental melodies, vocal prayers, and mystical chants have all been harnessed to establish communication with the Creator—uniting religious communities and articulating moral, political, social, and economic aspirations. Furthermore, these sacred sounds serve as the principal channel for invoking spirits. Many cultures believe that the utterance of specific sounds establishes a connection to all the elements present in the universe (Early, 2018).

Music and sound vibrations are employed to heal the body, mind, and spirit in certain belief systems. Within the vast spectrum of human expressive behaviors, the infusion of religious and spiritual convictions into oral poetry, chants, songs, and instrumental music is practiced by diverse peoples and cultures. This practice serves as an incredibly influential and inspirational way for these cultures to honor the presence of the Supreme in their lives.

The incorporation of religious music in meaningful ways has been witnessed in instances like civil rights movements, national liberation endeavors, and labor union picket lines. It's imperative to recognize that sacred sounds aren't confined solely to formal settings where religious rituals are enacted, although terms like "sacred" and "secular" are used to demarcate matters of the temporal and worldly from the realm of the universal and everlasting.

Sacred sounds also convey their profound beliefs by numerous other religious and spiritual traditions within diverse cultural communities. However, it's crucial to acknowledge that references to sacred sounds often conjure up familiar phrases such as "Make a joyful noise unto the Lord" or "Come before his presence with singing" (*New International Version*, 2011/1973, Psalm 100: 1-2), given the prevalence of the three Abrahamic faiths and their associated sacred texts in the United States.

For example, the Upanishads, ancient Vedic texts from India, emphasize that "the essence of sacred knowledge is word and sound, and the essence of word and sound is OM." This perspective underscores how even if the languages of various religious texts and spoken rituals might not be accessible to all cultural groups, sacred sounds remain universally understood as a medium through which diverse cultures honor higher states of wonder, consciousness, and order that transcend daily thoughts and actions, bridging a connection to the deeper fabric of the universe. As Plato eloquently noted, "music as moral law ... the essence of order, [that] leads to all that is good, just and beautiful, of which it is the invisible, but dazzling, passionate, and eternal form" (Early, 2018).

New hybrid worship spaces are being encountered by the world's religious cultures with physical migration and global communication. The exact worship location at different times is now shared by different religious services, while households are transmitted to by diverse religious practices and sacred music styles through radio and television broadcasts. These newfound encounters, which sometimes challenge established notions and open new vistas for religious and spiritual exploration, bring together previously isolated worship traditions.

For instance, how a traditional African-style service conducted by Ghanaian immigrants in a church context, replete with song, dance, drums, and modern instruments, evoked both discomfort and spiritual transcendence among long-standing parishioners was recounted by the Washington Post. It encapsulates a profound richness of human spirituality and expression when it comes to sacred sounds. People can engage with different worship services, festivals, and communities by immersing themselves in the diversity of sacred musical traditions, thereby fostering a deeper understanding of the shared human experience.

The vibrancy of these sacred sound traditions endures for future generations to appreciate and cherish, ensured by the preservation of them, documented through initiatives such as Folkways Records. The many ways humanity seeks to connect with the divine and grapple with the profound mysteries of existence are embraced by the realm of sacred sounds, which serves as an avenue for it.

## Gratitude and Appreciation

As adherents of the Abrahamic faith, we are called to fulfill various responsibilities: praying, demonstrating love for our neighbors, and contributing financially. Although these duties are widely recognized as integral parts of an Abrahamic life, many occasionally fall short. The busy nature of our lives, consumed by personal desires and worldly commitments, often overshadows our efforts to allocate time to nourish our spiritual connections. This observation also extends to our obligation to cultivate gratitude (Musick, n.d.).

The importance of expressing gratitude and being appreciative is consistently emphasized by the teachings within Abrahamic texts. However, by no means is leading a life brimming with gratitude an easy task. It demands a deliberate commitment, persistent dedication, and unwavering devotion, much like any other spiritual practice. Gratitude is not automatic; it necessitates a conscious effort, unlike fleeting emotions such as happiness or anger.

The instances where positivity has been bestowed upon us are required to be intentionally recognized by us. Feelings of gratitude tend to wane swiftly when we do not actively nurture it. For example, when we experience a minor ailment, such as a common cold, this sentiment rapidly dissipates, yet we might initially feel thankful for being in good health. Or yet we grumble about cooking, our kitchens are filled with an abundance of food, and yet we lament having "nothing to wear," our closets are brimming with clothing choices.

The advantages of gratitude and how we can foster higher levels of gratitude within ourselves have been dedicated significant time to understanding by psychologists studying moral development. Valuable perspectives on integrating gratitude as a spiritual discipline are contributed by this research combined with Abrahamic texts' insights. According to studies, with other emotions such as happiness or rage, thankfulness cannot be linked since, unlike these, it involves a purposeful and intentional choice (Musick, n.d.). This implies that to identify the actions or gestures that have benefited us, we must invest effort and time to truly experience gratitude.

To a moral compass, gratitude is often likened. As experts in psychology explain, "Psychologically, we have a lot of indicators" (Musick, n.d.). For threats, anxiety is an alert, while relational moments are indicated by gratitude (Musick, n.d.). Gratitude is a sign indicating that something positive has occurred and signaling acts of kindness and generosity. However, does it equate to embodying a life suffused with gratitude and experiencing occasional positive feelings? A distinction is suggested by research (Musick, n.d.).

To be a grateful person, feeling grateful is not equivalent. The goodness in their life is acknowledged by an individual who regularly embodies gratitude, and that it often originates from external sources is recognized by them. Factors that shape our propensity toward gratitude are identified by researchers: frequency, intensity, range, and density (Musick, n.d.). These factors gauge the depth of that sentiment, how frequently we experience gratitude, the number of elements that evoke gratitude simultaneously, and the number of people we appreciate for a single positive event.

For numerous things and toward many people, those strongly inclined toward gratitude experience more profound and frequent gratitude. While appearing straightforward, expressing gratitude for positive events or moments of good fortune implies there's something more profound fostering a disposition of gratitude, particularly within an Abrahamic context. Not solely thankful for blessings amidst challenging circumstances, it can also find gratitude in a genuinely grateful heart. Consider those who continue to exude gratitude and appreciation despite facing trials.

Several obstacles can obstruct the path to gratitude. Anxiety is a significant challenge, often rooted in a fear of intimacy that makes us reluctant to acknowledge dependency on others. Additionally, pride acts as a deterrent. When we believe we deserve our blessings, the motivation to express gratitude to others diminishes. Gratitude also necessitates a shift in thinking.

Often, we credit ourselves for the positive aspects of our lives and attribute adverse events to external factors. Gratitude disrupts this mindset by acknowledging the role others play in our success. It also challenges our desire to control our surroundings. Gratitude sometimes demands embracing life as it is and appreciating what we already have rather than striving for control.

Despite these challenges, the rewards of gratitude are substantial. Gratitude reinforces moral behavior and motivates both benefactors and recipients. Acts of kindness evoke gratitude, reinforcing the inclination to perform benevolent actions in the future. Gratitude also encourages recipients of kindness to reciprocate with acts of their own, creating a cycle of goodwill.

Gratitude fosters emotional and mental well-being while diminishing antisocial tendencies. It offers joy, balances negative emotions, and enhances our ability to derive pleasure from simple things. Gratitude contributes to improved sleep, reduced stress, and decreased physical discomfort. Those practicing gratitude often experience noticeable positive changes in friends and family.

Developing a grateful outlook is akin to mastering any skill requiring practice and commitment. Keeping a gratitude journal is a successful method of nurturing gratitude. By documenting daily occurrences that evoke gratitude, we learn to appreciate overlooked blessings. Studies show that keeping a gratitude journal enhances overall well-being, increases happiness and optimism, and improves physical health.

Expressing gratitude is also essential. Writing letters of gratitude, for instance, is a powerful practice. This exercise is integrated into psychology classes and has profound effects on us. By articulating gratitude, we affirm the goodness in life and learn the art of expressing appreciation.

Gratitude's benefits are firmly rooted in scientific research and Abrahamic texts' teachings (Musick, n.d.). Living with gratitude empowers us to embrace the good in life, transforming it into purposeful actions that enrich our lives and impact the world around us. Ultimately, gratitude directs our attention to the ultimate source of our blessings—divine love and grace.

The true test of gratitude lies in its capacity to inspire action. We not only stand to enjoy the countless advantages outlined via study by practicing thankfulness, but we also become acquainted with the multiplicity of ways God manifests Himself in the complexities of our lives. We learn to respect His sovereignty, mimic His moral character, and, perhaps most significantly, comprehend our value as receivers of His unfailing and ever-living grace.

# Conclusion

Throughout the journey we've embarked upon in the pages of this book, one resounding theme echoes loud and clear: the interconnectedness of the Abrahamic traditions.

We probed extensively into Judaism, Christianity, and Islam, unearthing not just contrasts but also significant common ideals that serve as the cornerstones of these faiths. And what we have discovered is this: These three faiths share more things in common than disparities.

From the reverence for family and community to the emphasis on compassion and justice, we've witnessed the harmonious chord that unites these traditions despite their distinct melodies. The key uniting factor is that all three of these religions hail the prophet Abraham as their patriarch.

Thus, when we take this into consideration, the three faiths are, in fact, cousins from the exact same family tree. There are differences in language and interpretations of the sacred texts, but the message remains one and the same. And that message, quite simply, is *love*!

We've uncovered a remarkable possibility for unity and understanding in the fabric of these Abrahamic faiths. We discovered similar connections underneath the surface that indicate our shared humanity. It serves as a reminder that, in our hearts, we are all explorers seeking connection, purpose, and meaning.

While the world tries to draw attention to our differences, these traditions encourage us to embrace the strands that bind us together, transcending boundaries and obstacles. So, as we conclude this book, I encourage you to carry these lessons with you like lights that enlighten your way.

Allow your understanding of these common ideals to motivate you to see the world through the eyes of unity and compassion. Infuse your engagements, choices, and relationships with the sagacity that beneath the surface, we are all linked by our shared humanity and the principles that unite us.

May these insights accompany you on your continual journey, gently reminding you of the profound interconnection that extends beyond faith and tradition.

As you stride forward, may you serve as an envoy of comprehension, a nurturer of harmony, a guiding light of empathy, and a spreader of love.

Your expedition, kindled by the melodious interplay of the Abrahamic traditions, holds the pledge of enriching not only your own life but the lives of those fortunate enough to cross your path.

Feel free to come back to its pages whenever you need a fresh perspective or a dose of inspiration.

As you venture forth, may your path be illuminated by the understanding, unity, and compassion we've uncovered together.

Until our paths converge once more, esteemed readers, may your journey be a tapestry woven with growth, inspiration, and the blessings that blossom from embracing the harmony of faith and spirituality within the Abrahamic traditions.

With heartfelt warmth and wishes for your onward spiritual voyage, God bless you and be with you always!

# Author's Bio

Allow me to introduce you to the captivating soul who brings life to these words: Meshari Alkulaib, a true wordsmith whose journey is as rich and diverse as the diversity of cultures he hails from.

With roots stretching from Kuwait to Bahrain, Los Angeles to Manchester, each strand contributes to the vibrant mosaic that colors his literary canvas.

His pen moves gracefully across pages, weaving tales that resonate with his multicultural adventures, inviting readers to step into vivid landscapes and meet characters as varied and vibrant as the world he inhabits.

Born on September 22, 1993, Meshari navigated his upbringing as an only child, an inquisitive traveler in pursuit of freedom, knowledge, and connection.

His hunger for wisdom, knowledge, and understanding took him into the world of academia, where he dived into medical studies at Bahrain's Royal College of Surgeons. That path peeled back layers of the human experience, revealing the intricate interconnectedness of life itself. But his curiosity wasn't contained within medicine's borders.

He then went on a wild ride, pursuing a second bachelor's degree in political science and government at California State University, Northridge. This twist in his journey opened up new horizons, sparking a fire for social justice and the tangled web of global dynamics.

Following his thirst for information, he found himself at the historic University of Manchester. There, he meticulously untangled the complex threads of human rights, securing a master's degree in the process. In the midst of Manchester's cobblestone streets, his dedication to nurturing understanding and embracing diversity was rooted even deeper, forming the bedrock of his impact as a writer.

At the time of writing this book, he was deep into his second year as a PhD student at the University of Manchester, plunging into the universe of Global Development. His exploration continues, navigating the intricate web of global challenges. But his influence doesn't end at the academic doorstep.

His words reverberate beyond, shining as a guiding light for hope, championing the values he holds close—the freedom to believe, speak, and stand by one's convictions.

Through his writing, he embarks on a journey that defies geographical boundaries, sparking conversations that connect cultures and break down societal barriers. Every stroke of his pen carries the purpose of sparking empathy, provoking thought, and etching an unforgettable mark on the hearts of readers across the globe.

As a writer, scholar, and advocate of peace, love, and justice among humankind, Meshari Alkulaib stands as living proof of words' immense power. His life's work embodies the ideals he fights for—unity, understanding, and the joy of embracing our shared humanity.

# References

Abdulsalam, M. (2006). *The tolerance of the Prophet toward other religions (part 2 of 2): Religious autonomy and politics, the tolerance of the Prophet toward other religions (part 1 of 2): To each their own religion*. The Religion of Islam. https://www.islamreligion.com/articles/207/viewall/tolerance-of-prophet-toward-other-religions/

*About us*. (2019). National Council of Churches. https://nationalcouncilofchurches.us/interreligious-relations-and-collaboration/interreligious-relations-with-a-focus-on-peace/

Abulafia, A. (2019, September 23). *The Abrahamic religions*. British Library. https://www.bl.uk/sacred-texts/articles/the-abrahamic-religions

*Ancient Jewish history: List of Jewish prophets*. (n.d.). Jewish Virtual Library. https://www.jewishvirtuallibrary.org/list-of-jewish-prophets

APU Edge Staff. (2021, April 14). *Humility as explored in religious, public and personal acts*. Edge. https://apuedge.com/humility-as-explored-in-religious-public-and-personal-acts/

*The arts of protection and healing in Islam: Water infused with blessing*. (2021, May 10). Ajam Media Collective. https://ajammc.com/2021/04/30/water-infused-with-blessing/

Bahri, C. (2023, May 22). *Understanding and practicing Islamic chants.* Complete Wellbeing. https://completewellbeing.com/article/understanding-islamic-chants/

Ballenger, M. (2017, February 19). *What does the bible say about personal responsibility?* Apply God's Word. https://applygodsword.com/what-does-the-bible-say-about-personal-responsibility/

Barton, K. (2013, August 12). *3 challenges facing Christianity today.* Conversant Faith. https://conversantfaith.com/2012/04/25/3-challenges-facing-christianity-today/

Barton, R. H. (2022, June 30). *What we believe about spiritual transformation.* Transforming Center. https://transformingcenter.org/2011/01/what-we-believe-about-spiritual-transformation/

Beliefnet. (2016, July 27). *Jewish healing practices.* Beliefnet.

Beyer, C. (2018, August 12). *Monotheistic religions of the world.* Learn Religions. https://www.learnreligions.com/monotheistic-religions-overview-95935

Brenner, M. (2017, September 28). *Islamic mosques & tombs.* Synonym. https://classroom.synonym.com/islamic-mosques-tombs-12085829.html

*Christianity: Celebrations and festivals.* (n.d.). URI. https://www.uri.org/kids/world-religions/christian-celebrations

Cohen, G. (n.d.). *Marginalization and expulsion*. Encyclopædia Britannica. https://www.britannica.com/topic/Judaism/Marginalization-and-expulsion

Cook, S. R. (2017, December 22). *The divine authorship of the bible archives*. Thinking on Scripture. https://thinkingonscripture.com/tag/the-divine-authorship-of-the-bible/

Cortez, J. (2018, June 22). *The importance of faith in the Christian life*. Biblical Christianity. https://biblical-christianity.com/tag/the-importance-of-faith-in-the-christian-life

*Differences and similarities in the Abrahamic faiths*. (2012, July 21). Redlands Daily Facts. https://www.redlandsdailyfacts.com/2012/07/21/differences-and-similarities-in-the-abrahamic-faiths/

Dobkowski, M. (n.d.). *Forgiveness and repentance in Judaism after the Shoah*. UTP Journals. https://utpjournals.press/doi/pdf/10.3138/uram.27.2.94

Early, J. (2018, October 19). *Sacred sounds: Belief & society*. Smithsonian Music. https://music.si.edu/story/sacred-sounds-belief-society

El Sayed, D. (2014). *Forgiveness in different religious traditions*. Love & Forgiveness in Governance. https://blogs.shu.edu/diplomacyresearch/2014/05/06/forgiveness-in-different-religious-traditions/

Farishta, H. (2020, June 1). *The concept of divine and human love in Islam.* TMV. https://themuslimvibe.com/faith-islam/the-concept-of-divine-and-human-love-in-islam

Farooqi, S. (2016, August 12). *Seeking guidance from the Quran.* Muslim Memo. https://muslimmemo.com/guidance-quran/

Fiedler, M. (2011, February 11). *Egypt, the Abrahamic traditions and social justice.* National Catholic Reporter. https://www.ncronline.org/blogs/ncr-today/egypt-abrahamic-traditions-and-social-justice

Fisch, T. (n.d.). *Rituals and sacraments.* University of St. Thomas. https://ir.stthomas.edu/cgi/viewcontent.cgi?article=1027&context=encounteringislam

Gnosis, I. (2015, December 9). *Judaism, Christianity & Islam: Forgotten shared beliefs of the Abrahamic faiths.* Ismaili Gnosis. https://ismailignosis.com/2015/12/09/judaism-christianity-islam-forgotten-shared-beliefs-of-the-abrahamic-faiths/

*God and prophets.* (2020, December 1). Cities of Light. https://www.islamicspain.tv/interfaith-coexistence/god-and-prophets/

Gold, R. S. (2022, November 3). *The power of Hebrew chant.* My Jewish Learning. https://www.myjewishlearning.com/article/the-power-of-hebrew-chant/

Gopin, M. (2002, April 25). *Patterns of Abrahamic reconciliation: Act, ritual, and symbol as transformation.* OUP Academic.

https://academic.oup.com/book/12864/chapter-abstract/163154614?redirectedFrom=fulltext

Gordis, R. D. (2019, January 8). *From belief to faith*. My Jewish Learning. https://www.myjewishlearning.com/article/from-belief-to-faith/

Gordon-Michaeli, L. (2019, October 7). *Taking self-reflection beyond Yom Kippur*. The Jewish News. https://www.thejewishnews.com/opinion/taking-self-reflection-beyond-yom-kippur/article_3ae722bb-3dd4-559e-9ada-eabe174af4b1.html

Grün, G. (2014, December 15). *What Christians, Jews and Muslims have in common*. DW Made for Minds. https://www.dw.com/en/faith-matters-7-things-christians-jews-and-muslims-share/a-18125302

Haarsma, D. (2018, May 3). *Universe or multiverse, God is still the creator*. BioLogos. https://biologos.org/articles/universe-or-multiverse-God-is-still-the-Creator

Habash, C. (2022, February 1). *What is self-reflection? why is self-reflection important?* Thriveworks. https://thriveworks.com/blog/importance-self-reflection-improvement/

Harris, A. (2021, January 28). *Judaism and the challenges of modern life*. Shalom Hartman Institute. https://www.hartman.org.il/judaism-and-the-challenges-of-modern-life/

Hegarty, S. (2020, January 21). *From smiling at strangers to feeding those in need: What different faiths say about kindness.* ABC Everyday. https://www.abc.net.au/everyday/five-religious-australians-reflect-on-kindness-and-faith/11852608

Hhteam. (2016, October 23). *Mystical Christianity: Rituals and spiritual practice II.* Humanity Healing Network. http://humanityhealing.net/2012/04/rituals-spiritual-practices-mystical-christianity-ii/

*The Holy Quran: Text, translation & commentary.* (2016). Kitab Bhavan.

Hoffman, M. (2017, December 22). *Wedding traditions across the Abrahamic faiths.* Jewish News Syndicate. https://www.jns.org/wedding-traditions-across-the-abrahamic-faiths-2

*How religion strengthens community: Chats, up for discussion.* Zócalo Public Square. (2020, July 11). https://www.zocalopublicsquare.org/2010/10/19/how-religion-strengthens-community/ideas/up-for-discussion/

Huda. (2018, May 4). *What Muslims believe about prophets.* Learn Religions. https://www.learnreligions.com/prophets-of-islam-2004542

Huda. (2019, May 4). *5 Muslim daily prayer times and what they mean.* Learn Religions. https://www.learnreligions.com/islamic-prayer-timings-2003811

*Importance of reflection and taking stock of oneself.* (2017, January 8). Islam Question & Answers. https://islamqa.info/en/answers/248273/importance-of-reflection-and-taking-stock-of-oneself

*Interfaith dialogue between Abrahamic religions.* (2020, November 24). The Leimena Institute. https://leimena.org/eng/interfaith-dialogue-between-abrahamic-religions/

Ismail, Z. ibn. (2022, May 12). *6 Islamic festivals and holidays.* The Quran Recital. https://thequranrecital.com/what-festivals-do-muslims-celebrate/

Jacobs, R. J. (2021, December 14). *Jewish attitudes toward poverty.* My Jewish Learning. https://www.myjewishlearning.com/article/jewish-attitudes-toward-poverty/

*Judaism: Celebrations and festivals.* (n.d.). URI. https://www.uri.org/kids/world-religions/jewish-celebrations

Kayahan, A. B. (2016, December 28). *How funeral traditions differ across Abrahamic religions.* Daily Sabah. https://www.dailysabah.com/feature/2016/12/29/how-funeral-traditions-differ-across-abrahamic-religions

Khan, N. K. (2020, February 4). *Divine duty: Islam and social justice.* Yaqeen Institute for Islamic Research. https://yaqeeninstitute.org/read/paper/divine-duty-islam-and-social-justice

Kihlander, K. (2022, November 3). *What each major religion says about animal rights.* Sentient Media.

https://sentientmedia.org/what-each-major-religion-says-about-animal-rights/

Lewis, A. (2019, August 13). *Worship as a communal experience.* CPH Blog - Concordia Publishing House. https://blog.cph.org/worship/worship-as-a-communal-experience

Libenson, D. (2021, February 4). *Akedah project.* Sefaria Collections. https://www.sefaria.org/collections/akedah-project?tab=sheets

Lillibridge, L. (2023, January 30). *8 ways to trust your intuition or Inner Wisdom.* Everyday Power. https://everydaypower.com/trust-your-intuition/

Mallery, L. (2022, January 11). *Challenges faced by Muslim youth in the West.* About Islam. https://aboutislam.net/reading-islam/living-islam/challenges-faced-by-muslim-youth-in-the-west/

Mindel, N. *The three daily prayers.* (n.d.). Chabad.org https://www.chabad.org/library/article_cdo/aid/682091/jewish/The-Three-Daily-Prayers.htm

Moore, J. & Turkel, N. (2020, June 25). *Jews, Muslims & Christians are being persecuted, and it must stop now.* Newsweek. https://www.newsweek.com/jews-muslims-christians-are-all-persecuted-europe-it-must-stop-now-opinion-1513249

Mufti, I. (2013, May 27). *Core values of Islam.* The Religion of Islam.

https://www.islamreligion.com/articles/10256/core-values-of-islam/

Musick, T. (n.d.). *What good is gratitude? The role of Thanksgiving in personal development.* Point Loma Nazarene University. https://www.pointloma.edu/resources/counseling-psychology/what-good-gratitude-role-thanksgiving-personal-development

*New International Version.* (2011). New International Version Bible Online. https://www.biblegateway.com/versions/New-International-Version-NIV-Bible/ (Original work published in 1973)

Nielson, S. (2017, May 27). *7 ways to pray with sincerity—part 1.* Prayer A to Z. https://studyingprayer.com/2017/05/27/7-ways-to-pray-with-sincerity-part-1/

Oates, J. (2019, December 13). *Discipleship vs. mentorship: How they differ & are similar.* Just Disciple. https://justdisciple.com/discipleship-mentorship/

ORBC Family (2021, June 18). *7 different types of prayer in the Bible.* Oak Ridge Baptist Church. https://www.orbcfamily.org/blog/prayer/7-different-types-of-prayer-in-the-bible/

*Peacemaking 101: Biblical conflict resolution.* (2021, September 17). Pastor Resources. https://pastorresources.com/peacemaking-101-biblical-conflict-resolution/

Peach, D. (n.d.). *What does a spiritual mentor do in the life of a Christian?* What Christians Want To Know RSS. https://www.whatchristianswanttoknow.com/what-does-a-spiritual-mentor-do-in-the-life-of-a-christian/

*Pilgrimage in different religions.* (2022, June 20). IslamOnline. https://islamonline.net/en/pilgrimage-in-different-religions/

Plante, T. (2009, November 8). *Meditative practices from the many religious traditions.* Psychology Today. https://www.psychologytoday.com/us/blog/do-the-right-thing/200911/meditative-practices-from-the-many-religious-traditions

Prabhu, L. (2008, February 14). *Christian chants: Styles, features and benefits.* Complete Wellbeing. https://completewellbeing.com/article/christian-chants/

*Prophets of God. Chapter 9.* (2011, January 1). The Church of Jesus Christ of Latter-Day Saints. https://www.churchofjesuschrist.org/study/manual/gospel-principles/chapter-9-prophets-of-god?lang=eng

Puchalski, C. (1970, January 1). *Spiritual care in health care: Guideline, models, spiritual assessment and the use of the©FICA spiritual history tool.* SpringerLink. https://link.springer.com/chapter/10.1007/978-3-030-70139-0_3

*The Quran* (M. A. S. Abdel Haleem, Trans.) (2010). Oxford University Press.

*Quran: Divine authorship or authored by men?* (2019, March 19). Christian Publishing House Blog. https://christianpublishinghouse.co/2019/03/19/quran-divine-authorship-or-authored-by-men/

*Rites and ceremonies.* (n.d.). Patheos. https://www.patheos.com/library/christianity/ritual-worship-devotion-symbolism/rites-and-ceremonies

*Rites of passage.* (n.d.). Israel & Judaism Studies (IJS). https://www.ijs.org.au/rites-of-passage/

*Ritual purification.* (n.d.). The Spiritual Life. https://slife.org/ritual-purification/

*Sacred space.* (n.d.). Patheos. https://www.patheos.com/library/islam/ritual-worship-devotion-symbolism/sacred-space

Salkin, J. (2018, June 3). *The three little words that Jews never say.* Religion News Service. https://religionnews.com/2017/02/14/valentines-day-god-love-judaism-christianity/

*Self love: The importance of learning to Love yourself.* (2019, January 25). Seattle Christian Counseling. https://seattlechristiancounseling.com/articles/self-love-importance-learning-love

Sharma, P. (2022, January 5). *Sor1 - core ethical teachings of Judaism.* HSCOne. https://hsc.one/post/core-ethical-teachings-judaism/

Sherwood, H. (2020, November 15). *Religious intolerance is 'bigger cause of prejudice than race', says report.* The Guardian.

https://www.theguardian.com/world/2020/nov/15/religious-intolerance-is-bigger-cause-of-prejudice-than-race-says-report

Shmelova, M. (2023, July 28). *Let's discover the symbols of Jewish culture and architecture—the activity path.* TupTupTup.org.pl. https://tuptuptup.org.pl/en/symbols-of-jewish-culture-and-architecture/

Silberberg, C. (2012). *Why do I need a spiritual mentor?* Chabad.org. https://www.chabad.org/library/article_cdo/aid/1777641/jewish/Why-Do-I-Need-a-Spiritual-Mentor.htm

Singh, C. G. (2012, October 18). *Nature: The source of Inspiration.* Speaking Tree. https://www.speakingtree.in/blog/nature-the-source-of-inspiration

Spain, D. (2017, December 12). *The 3 main roles of spiritual leaders.* DEREK SPAIN. https://derekspain.com/2014/09/25/the-3-main-roles-of-spiritual-leaders/

*Spiritual discipline in Judaism.* (n.d.). What-When-How. https://what-when-how.com/love-in-world-religions/spiritual-discipline-in-judaism/

Stacey, A. (2023, June 28). *Ishmael & Isaac—story of great brothers and prophets.* About Islam. https://aboutislam.net/reading-islam/understanding-islam/ishmael-and-isaac-great-brothers-and-prophets/

Studzinski, J. (2022, April 17). *The three Abrahamic faiths celebrating festivals have an important and holy task ahead.* LinkedIn. https://www.linkedin.com/pulse/three-abrahamic-faiths-celebrating-festivals-have-holy-studzinski

Subhani, J. S. (n.d.). *The Islamic moral system: Tafsir—commentary of Surah Al-Hujarat (49).* Al Islam. https://www.al-islam.org/islamic-moral-system-tafsir-commentary-surah-al-hujarat-49-jafar-subhani

Telloian, C. (2021, March 1). *Depression treatment: Therapy, medication, and coping strategies.* PsychCentral. https://psychcentral.com/depression/depression-treatment#next-steps

*The Torah.* (1996). Easton Press.

*Three natural miracles.* (2013). Chabad.org. https://www.chabad.org/parshah/article_cdo/aid/46079/jewish/Three-Natural-Miracles.htm

*Torah.* (n.d.). New World Encyclopedia. https://www.newworldencyclopedia.org/entry/Torah

*Uri kids: World religions.* (n.d.). URI. https://www.uri.org/kids/world-religions

van Baaren, T. (2023). *Monotheism.* Encyclopædia Britannica. https://www.britannica.com/topic/monotheism

Wahlberg, M. (2020, July 17). *Divine revelation.* Stanford Encyclopedia of Philosophy. https://plato.stanford.edu/entries/divine-revelation/

*What can you do against prejudice?* (2020, February 24). Anne Frank Website. https://www.annefrank.org/en/topics/prejudice-and-stereotypes/what-can-you-do-against-prejudice/

*What does the Bible say about Christian values and Christian life?* (n.d.). https://www.christianbiblereference.org/faq_Christian Values.htm

*What does the Bible say about compassion?* (2011, August 24). Got Questions. https://www.gotquestions.org/Bible-compassion.html

White, L. (2022, July 27). *5 Christian principles that will help your relationships*. Beliefnet. https://www.beliefnet.com/love-family/relationships/galleries/5-christian-principles-that-will-help-your-relationships.aspx

Wynne, M. (2020, June 5). *The ancient or original meaning of the Holy Cross*. Synonym. https://classroom.synonym.com/ancient-original-meaning-holy-cross-5476.html

Younus, R. & Soto, C. (2021, July 27). *Native and Muslim Americans face challenges engaging philanthropy*. Johnson Center for Philanthropy. https://johnsoncenter.org/blog/native-and-muslim-americans-two-marginalized-communities-find-similar-hurdles-in-engaging-philanthropy/

Zohery, A. (2022, September 29). *The kindness of Prophet Muhammad (s)*. IslamiCity.

https://www.islamicity.org/6428/the-kindness-of-prophet-muhammad-s/

Printed in Great Britain
by Amazon